THE JAPANESE
EDUCATIONAL
CHALLENGE

THE JAPANESE EDUCATIONAL CHALLENGE

A Commitment to Children

Merry White

THE FREE PRESS
A Division of Macmillan, Inc.
NEW YORK

Collier Macmillan Publishers
LONDON

The Free Press
A Division of Macmillan, Inc.
866 Third Avenue, New York, N.Y. 10022

Collier Macmillan Canada, Inc.

Printed in the United States of America

printing number

1   2   3   4   5   6   7   8   9   10

Library of Congress Cataloging-in-Publication Data

White, Merry I.
   The Japanese educational challenge.

   Bibliography: p.
   Includes index.
   1. Education—Japan—1965-   . 2. Education—
Japan—Aims and objectives.   I. Title.
LA1312.W44   1987   370'.952   86-29503
ISBN 0-02-933800-X

For Jenny and Ben

CONTENTS

PREFACE AND ACKNOWLEDGMENTS

This book was written out of years of experience and observation in Japan. My interest in Japanese children, parents, and teachers began with my undergraduate years when my advisors, Professors John Pelzel and Beatrice Whiting, urged me to write a thesis on the historical development of the relationship between the Japanese student and teacher. Twenty-five years later, I am still interested in the same relationship.

That subject now captures the imagination of many others besides parents and teachers in Japan and the West. How Japanese children learn, in the family and at school, now represents something wider than an academic concern with Asian tradition, bureaucracy, and test score outcomes.

I am grateful to many more people than I can mention here. My interest in Japanese education also took shape in my doctoral dissertation, and my advisors, Professors Ezra Vogel and Yoshihiro Shimizu, provided significant impetus. Later, at the Harvard Graduate School of Education's Project on Human Potential, a grand and leisurely examination of learning across many fields and cultures was made possible. This gave me the chance to consider again the role of culture in Japanese education. Robert LeVine encouraged me to delve more deeply into the meaning of goals for the Japanese child, and his insightful observations both here and in Japan helped to spur my thinking. Other colleagues such as Howard Gardner, Israel Scheffler, and Patricia Graham were helpful and supportive. Lois Taniuchi Peak has worked with me since the earliest days of the Project, and I owe her much, for her intellectual contributions and for her friendship.

Other colleagues and friends, further afield, who have contributed to my understanding include: Wakako Hironaka, Catherine Lewis, Thomas Rohlen, Ronald Dore, Kunio Wakai, Joseph Tobin, William Cummings, Takeo Doi, Akira Hoshino, Sumiko Iwao, Michiko Fuka-zawa, and Kazuyuki Kitamura. Others who helped me in Japan were Shigefumi Nagano and Hiroshi Kida, as well as the many school and ministry of education officials who gave me their time as well as opportunities to visit schools. Tadano Sagara, whose *juku* (after school class) I visited, has my special thanks.

Sachiko and Yoshimitsu Ide and their children, Lisa and Corky, have spent many hours over the past twenty-five years talking with me about our children and each other's societies. Their help and friendship I value very highly.

I would also like to thank the friends who have provided counsel and solace: Leonie Gordon, Susan Pollak, Mitzi Goheen, Steve Fjell-man, Jean Jackson, Leslie Swartz, Kathy Hartford, Tom Levenson, and Henry Smith. George Rowland at The Free Press shepherded the book, and me, through its final stages with great skill and good humor.

It is customary to thank one's editor, but in this case my thanks to Grant Ujifusa extend beyond custom. Grant frequently invoked the presence of his Japanese grandmother, and that image, together with his own enthusiasm and consummate skills in the making of a book, kept me centered and eager, the very model of a Japanese student. None of the above, even Grant's grandmother, bears any responsibility for errors of fact and point of view, which remain mine.

THE JAPANESE
EDUCATIONAL
CHALLENGE

INTRODUCTION

A Children's Paradise?

My eight-year-old son, Ben, assumes Japan would be paradise for a child: he covets all the Japanese robot toys, eschewing American imitations. His favorite photograph is a panoramic shot of the Keio department store's toy department in Tokyo. He knows of Boys' Day (May 5), Girls' Day (March 3), and the ceremonial "7–5–3" Day in November when children of these ages are taken to Shinto temples to be presented for blessings. He wonders why children here aren't so singled out for special attention.

But the Japanese child who spent a year at Ben's school puzzles my son. Why is the Asian child so capable in some things, so polite and well mannered, so able to get along well with adults and speak up in a clear and forthright manner in class but so unassertive? My son asked, "Why is he so good?" Is Taroo afraid of being punished? Does the Japanese child get spanked? Ben thinks so, and assumes that Taroo is good because threatening adults have made him submit. My eight-year-old cannot put the pieces together: perhaps Japan isn't a child's paradise after all.

The puzzle of Japanese childhood has entered the mainstream of public debate, having even been called "evidence" in the rhetoric of the trade war. American observers note that Japanese education and child-rearing techniques probably have something to do with the high quality of imported automobiles. And, when Japanese children

1

test higher in math and science than any others in the world, the battleground of competition seems to be shifting to schools. The subject of internal criticism and movements for reform for much of the post-Sputnik era, education in the West now seems to face a new "Sputnik": the Japanese child, as goad, goal, and measure of success.

The visible outcomes of Japanese education and child rearing include stunning literacy rates, a highly sophisticated general population, and a well-socialized and committed work force. Less than 0.7 percent of the Japanese population is illiterate, compared to 20 percent in the United States. An example of the uniform effects of education may be seen on ordinary television news broadcasts: the level of discourse, sophisticated analyses of facts and figures, and general tone of reporting is striking, approximated only on some American "educational television." Furthermore, this sophistication is not restricted to the upper socioeconomic strata. A worker on the factory floor can understand graphs, charts, and other symbolic notations, and work with complex mathematical formulas. The implications are obvious for American plant foremen, teachers, and parents alike. Japanese parents and schools act in concert to produce a remarkable outcome.

Of course, Western observers portray the Japanese child, his experiences and his talents, selectively. The images are psychologically projective and self-protective. Our media show a photo of a Japanese child sitting at a desk, in a well-ordered row, wearing a white headband marked with red and black characters exhorting him to struggle on. He is shown either raising his hand fervently or writing with furled-brow concentration, the picture of intensity. The image is designed to evoke history as well as to imply the future: this child is the kamikaze pilot of his generation, hell-bent on Japanese supremacy, and the world will be his unless we wake up to the peril he symbolizes.

But what would we do if we did "wake up"? For we are told that Japanese educational successes are the product of an inhuman regime of forced-march study and that childhood as we know it does not exist in Japan: the playgrounds are empty, mothers are homework tyrants; weekends and vacations are devoted to organized study. The culmination of childhood's toils, we are told, is the examination. Success means entry into the industrial machine, and the child who gets into a top university becomes the ultimate "economic animal." Failure is shame and may lead to death: the juvenile suicide rate is seen to be tied to academic shortcoming. The "awakened" Western observer, confronted with this understanding of Japanese childhood, would scarcely choose to emulate it. The personal and national costs are too high. Accordingly, we want to believe that Japanese education is dehumanizing and unfair, both to Japanese children and to the American economy.

But parents and teachers who have witnessed problems in our schools, the alienation and lack of motivation among our students, are aware that Western schools are not serving our postindustrial society very well. They look for programs of reform or for improvement in our educational environments and for models and ideas outside the American mainstream.

Meanwhile, the diversity of our educational experience offers no single solution: "free" schools, fundamentalist religious schools, "back to basics" programs, "open classrooms," elite prep schools, and John Dewey–derived "progressive schools." Then there is the ordinary school, which, avoiding ideology and even explicit pedagogies, limps along, hoping to keep order and get through the day. All these types of schools may educate our children, to varying degrees, but they provide no coherent standards for all children, and in any case, the best education is available only to a small percentage of our society.

As in the case of corporate managers and economic theorists, however, it is all too easy for would-be educational reformers to look to Japan for a new blueprint. Executives rush to Japan, fill their travel diaries with tips on how to manage employee relationships, and leave feeling they have found the secrets of Japan's industrial might. Similarly, teachers and school administrators embark on sojourns that include three days of classroom visits, an overnight stay in a Zen temple, a trip to a hot spring, and meetings with Japanese teachers and school officials—all these are only "mutual admiration" ceremonies. And it is just as hard to put to work the "secrets" these teachers think they now have as it is to bring quality control back to America, where it originated.

What is to be done, then, if Japan is really neither a diabolically clever competitor nor the answer to our prayers? Our deep concern with our own children's lives and our fascination with Japan can be used creatively *if* we do *not* look for the "quick fix" or insist upon cut-and-paste borrowing. For example, simply increasing our present 180 school days per year to 240 is no guarantee that our children will benefit.

We need to understand the Japanese schools and the experience of the Japanese child as rooted in deep psychological and cultural realities; in borrowing European and American models of schooling Japan did *not* borrow Western conceptions of learning and childhood. In Japan, to be modern is not, in any pervasive sense, to be Western. To look at Japan as a "Western" country only leads to a shock of *nonrecognition.* Our contemporary interest in Japan must not lead us to think that there is only one way to succeed, to be "modern." So I will *not* present Japan as a strict model for us to follow. The message of Japanese parenting, schooling, and social cohesion is neither that they are unique and inimitable nor that we can directly translate their secrets into American terms, but rather that there exist in the world today many modes, a diversity of possibilities, in fact, for the development of children.

What we need most is a consensus among parents, teachers, and policymakers that permits a more open view of our own educational system and the cultural conceptions that underlie it. We, too, have "culture," however hard it is to see it, that shapes our ideas of what a child is, how he may be educated, and what goals we have for his future.[1]

Western ideals of and for the child come out of our history and bear the residue of the Enlightenment, the Rousseauian romance of the primitive, and the sentimentalism of the Victorian era. Americans also take very seriously the Founding Fathers' principles of independence, equality, and individualism. The sum of these influences implies that (1) the child is vulnerable and therefore to be protected; (2) the child is potentially a rational creature and therefore to be educated; (3) the child is naturally creative and beautiful by nature and therefore not to be constrained; (4) the child has rights of free choice and equal access to the goods of life and therefore must be protected by law. Finally, the child is a member of society, but here the consequences for his upbringing are not so clear, and it is also here that Japanese child-rearing may indeed be instructive.

What kind of school nurtures such a child, whose nature is individual and whose spirit must be free? Whatever it is, that school must also teach him what is to be learned, and one of the things he must learn is that he must cheerfully conform to the community's expectations and yield some exercise of free choice to the necessary constraints of society. If "society" is simply to be seen as the social environment in which the child is nurtured and developed only as an individual, the child's active participation in and responsibility toward it is less important than if his social environment is a "community" in which his identity and future life chances are embedded. While they are in fact communities, Western schools do not generally stress communal values, but provide an ambivalent educational context that reflects various ideological precepts. And yet a few universals do span all cultures, and one is close to omnipresent: the understanding that adults are responsible for children's lives and that society at large can help to develop an appropriate environment for learning and development. Later we will explore the implications of the universals and the differences more fully.

This book traces the lives of children in Japan from conception through the high school years and into the university. Through observation, interview analysis, and vignettes of individual children at various grade levels, I try to shape an understanding of childhood as experienced by the child himself and shaped by social institutions and cultural norms. I hope that this approach will show Japanese children not as programmed automata but as ordinary kids—but ordinary *Japanese* kids, whose parents, teachers, and society believe in learning and will accordingly help children engage wholeheartedly, and for the most part pleasurably, in their work, whether that effort leads to a life of bureaucratic predictability, small-shop retailing, or breakthrough innovations.

Naturally, I will be comparing the experiences of childhood in Japan and Western countries. The comparisons will for the most part be explicit, but it is well to warn the reader that implicit contrasts lurk as well. Where explicit, any comparing done may be risky, since general statements may not represent the case for all Western children vis-à-vis all Japanese children, especially the former.

For the term "Western," the major point of reference is the United States, but comparisons between Japan and European countries are also pertinent. Whereas the United States and Japan, on many social dimensions, represent polar opposites, bringing in a European country for comparison reduces the sense of "uniqueness" attributed to Japanese society and culture. But because mutual fascination exists between the United States and Japan, and because our educational systems are tied together historically, the need to stress points of similarity and divergence in these two countries has become a practical as well as an intellectual requirement.

A child engaged in his learning, and the home relationships and groups that create and support that engagement, may be the single most significant measure of successful education. In Japan it is not overstating the case to say that life is the life of the group first and foremost. It is also a life judged and supported by a social consensus that establishes standards for performance and behavior.

Hence Japanese society is governed by consensus rather than by ideological abstractions: "isms" in no way prevail, and morality is never couched in terms of black-and-white commandments. For example, unlike morality in the West, Japanese interpersonal morality is much more broadly understood than that implied universal balance of the Golden Rule. What you do unto others is not necessarily going to be paid back in kind by those same others, but rather, over time, a balance of reciprocity between parent and child, between patron and artist, between teacher and student, is created through obligations and expressions of kindness that are not reckoned by tomorrows but may take generations. And there is no one way of living that constitutes proper behavior, consideration, and sensitivity to others, but several, depending on the situation and the specific relationship. Accordingly, Westerners often believe that Japanese "polite behavior" is shallow and insincere. Furthermore, since the rules seem inconsistent, Westerners often feel very suspicious of such behavior and sometimes revert to propagandistic stereotypes of the two-faced, untrustworthy Japanese.

At the root of the problem is a very different concept of self and its relationship to the group. The Western, and particularly the American, view of the self is that it must be consistent and unitary and that any expression of regard for others must be constant and straightforward, "up front." We "wear our hearts on our sleeves," at least ideally, and regard inconsistency as hypocrisy or shiftiness.

The Japanese concept of the good person does not insist upon such uniformity and allows for a more complex relationship with the social environment. Not only does the Japanese language demand a range of levels of address depending on the speaker's relationship to his or her listener, but behavior is similarly calibrated. Hence there are areas of freedom in the wider society and the deepest recesses of the most personal "self" that most Westerners cannot fathom.

Children are taught to understand the differences in expectations and standards as they learn to speak and as their circle of acquaintance broadens. They are also provided with support and protection for the "personal self" that is not affected by the "situationalism" of the "public self." Thus, to live up to the standards enforced by the

Japanese social consensus one does have to be a good group member, but one does not yield autonomy to a faceless mass. Instead, measuring up means a confirmation of identity-conferring membership, in which the private and public selves are both honored.

This book treats psychocultural, historical, and social conceptions that create the environment in which Japanese children experience life. Part I shows Japan to be a society committed to children and to education. The commitment exists at all levels of Japanese society and among all its institutions. Education is seen as key to industrial development, national cohesion, international political stature, personal development, moral character-building, cultural continuity, and the creation and maintenance of interpersonal relationships. Chapter 1 reviews the national mood toward children, and presents the views of parents, educators, politicians, and the media. Chapter 2 outlines Japanese psychological concepts related to child rearing and learning and shows how mothers and teachers provide motivation and incentive. The "good child" and the "good mother" as the Japanese understand them are set forth. Chapter 3 presents the history of schooling, from pre-modern times to the present, and traces the development of the Japanese educational system from indigenous and borrowed models. Chapter 4 provides an overview of the contemporary system and educational practices. The training, role, and experiences of teachers are treated in Chapter 5.

Part II examines learning at home and at school. Chapter 6 presents the earliest years of childhood, especially the relationship of child and mother from birth to the beginnings of formal schooling. We see a three-year-old about to enter nursery school, and his mother's preparations for an entrance into this new world. Chapter 7 presents teachers and children in the elementary schools, as exemplified by the school and home lives of a third and sixth grader. Chapter 8 takes on secondary schools and the impact of examinations on the lives of children in junior high and high school. We see both the hard-driven achiever and the child whose path will not take him to Tokyo University.

Part III looks at needs and goals in education in the West and Japan, and, in the current climate of educational reform, analyzes the problems of transferring practices from one society to another. Chapter 9 gives an overview of goals and issues in contemporary Japanese educational reform. Japanese critiques of their own schools are examined. Finally, in chapter 10 the rhetoric and the realities of learning from Japanese practices are presented, and larger questions about Western goals and means in our children's education are raised.

If there is anything to be learned from looking at the lives of other people's children, it is that while we all want the best for our children, that "best" is differently construed in Japan and the means to develop it are also not our own. What emerges from reflection on experiences of Japanese childhood are the following conclusions: Japan's modern schools, like Japan's modern society, are modern but not Western; Japanese children are motivated to learn in ways which are not a part of Western psychology; Japanese support for children and learning is the major, if not obsessive, focus throughout the society. The answer, therefore, is that we should hold Japan up as a mirror, not as a blueprint.

Yet what specifically the West can learn from Japan is an open question. We can, to be sure, learn more about Japan, and in doing so, as I have just said, learn more about ourselves. Japanese advances of the last twenty years were based on American principles of productivity, not on samurai skills and zen austerities. Therefore, looking for mysterious Japanese secrets, or worse, complaining about Japanese modes as inhuman or unfair, will not get us very far. If nothing else, the Japanese have shown they can adjust programs and policies to the needs and resources of the times. We must do the same. We need to regain the scientific literacy we have lost and reacquire concrete skills and participatory social techniques.

In short, we should see Japan as having established a new standard, not as having provided a model to be emulated. To match that standard we have our own version of general excellence, according to which we need to develop a long view, consistent with our own cultural values and goals. Our children's education will then be the beneficiary.

PART I

A SOCIETY MOBILIZED FOR EDUCATION

1

RESOURCES AND MOBILIZATION

A Backdrop for the Centrality of Education in Japan

In Japan the care of children is not regarded as just a domestic concern. Indeed the entire nation is mobilized behind children and their education. This national obsession may well be responsible for children Western parents and educators would be proud of, children whose lives and future prospects meet our standards of approval. In short, the Japanese national engagement in child development is something we should envy.

What has fueled the drive to maximize the life chances of children? How does the intense commitment to children mirror the nation's conception of its past, present, and future?

THE SCARCITY SYNDROME

Japanese have several phrases that roll smoothly off tongues to "explain" their society to others. Prominent among these are: "a narrow island country," "low in natural resources," "vulnerable to enemies, earthquakes, and fires." The self-conscious insistence on Japan's fragility and accompanying low profile has in recent years

11

met with some foreign criticism as trade officials and international aid agencies ask Japanese business and government to take a more responsible role in the world economy and in developing countries. Japanese business, no longer completely self-effacing, has to some extent responded with greater confidence, while Prime Minister Yasuhiro Nakasone is hardly a shrinking violet. Nevertheless the urgency that drives the Japanese "path of pure endeavor" is still based on a sense of precarious deficiency. And this is more than a historical residue from times when Japan suffered real scarcity. Among the Japanese a conviction that they are living on the very edge is a driving cultural force that shapes not only industrial process and international negotiation, but also lies at the core of household management and parent–child relationships.

Japanese scholar Sumiko Iwao demonstrates historical perspective on the "scarcity syndrome" when she analyzes women's strategies for family and business management.[1] A century ago, at the time of the Meiji Restoration, 80 percent of Japan's population worked and lived on farms. Agricultural practices and development were constrained by limited arable land, given the high proportion of mountainous terrain. Hence the arable coastal areas were densely populated by farmers who had to operate small-scale farms, utilizing every square inch of available land. Furthermore, agricultural production could not be counted upon since Japan's climate is marked by dramatic and damaging typhoons, flooding during the rainy season, and unpredictable, unseasonable changes in temperature. In sum, the traditional Japanese farmer was tied to a precarious venture, and success required extreme industriousness to overcome the sometimes catastrophic losses incurred during periods of hardship.

Hard work was accompanied by a need for short-term and long-term planning, by a continual, adaptive refinement of strategies and alternatives, and this mind-set has persisted to the present. One strategy that Iwao cites as especially evident among women is that of self-abnegation, denial, and sacrifice, in service not to masochism, but to a greater long-term good for themselves and their families. Going without (and letting others know about it) is of course a common way for women everywhere to acquire virtue. But Japanese women have developed the production of guilt in others into a transcendent cultural art form.

Using arts of sacrifice and management women acted as the chief distribution agents in the household. As Iwao says, "their ingenuity and creativity in controlling and husbanding the family's resources gave women a sense of responsibility, freedom and self-expression which was unique to their situation.''[2]

Making a virtue of necessity may well have been the crucial skill in Japanese development. The cultural choices made that allowed people to see advantages in scarcity meant that Japanese did more than *cope* with deprivation. Mothers and national leaders alike employed a consciousness that scarcity imperiled, and vigilance had to be constantly maintained—lest a deadening fatalism replace energies aroused through the agency of impending doom.

Meanwhile children were seen as a scarce resource, since infant mortality rates were very high. Moreover, children were greatly valued because they represented the continuity of the family and the security of parents in old age. They also provided labor for the family, and by the age of twelve were able to participate fully in agricultural and domestic chores. They might finally enhance the family's virtue and status in the community by becoming students who did well in school.

Education itself was regarded as a scarce resource, since it was not universally available and since most children of farm families would attend school for only a few years. Needs of the farm took precedence over education, and at certain times of the year there were few children in rural schools. As in China, the culture of origin for much of Japan's pre-modern education, learning did not provide occupational credentials because work was inherited along with land and interclass mobility was slight. Nevertheless, learning and the moral advantage it symbolized was hard-won and greatly valued.

That moral advantage has today been largely superseded by the power of academic credentials to secure an occupational future. Still, school achievement is seen to confirm a high level of virtue in the student and his supporting family. This Confucian-based virtue, an important social resource itself, is now available to all, but the road to it is difficult: in fact, if anything comes easily in Japan, it does not confer virtue. As we will see, one important result of a child's educational experience is the ability to commit intense effort to a task, and that devotion to hard work itself is the mark of virtue.

Accordingly, deep parental investment in children begins early and continues through high school years. Mothers are intensely committed to their children from the onset of pregnancy and see their major life's task as the rearing of successful children. Mothers are always looking for innovative ways to enhance their children's life chances. For example, in Riverdale, New York, where there is a sizable Japanese population, school administrators recently noticed that Japanese families were purchasing two sets of textbooks for each child. They soon discovered that one set was for the mother, who would study one or more lessons ahead of her child to help him or her in schoolwork. The result was that Japanese children who entered school in September knowing little or no English often finished in June at the top of the class in all subjects.

JAPAN AT RISK

The Japanese see themselves at risk not only from scarcity but from cataclysm, and doomsday is a recurrent cultural symbol. The plot of a recent best-selling novel, *Nihon Chinbotsu* (The Sinking of Japan), is based on the ultimate disaster. Thanks to a succession of earthquakes and tidal waves, the main islands of the Japanese archipelago are sinking gradually into the sea. Soon to lose their motherland, the population is mobilized by the government to emigrate—in a supremely well planned exodus, of course—to several other parts of the world. Some choose (or are forced) to go down with the ship, but most find themselves tussling with the complexities of social and technological engineering. This is a suggestive disaster novel, which tells us much about how the Japanese view the fragility of their national identity.

And this fragility is as frequently invoked or implied as disaster or scarcity. Racial purity, though not explicitly apostrophized, is an important concern, as is cultural homogeneity. Koreans and *burakumin,* the former outcast group, are ghettoized and restricted—though racially hard to distinguish from "pure Japanese." Those away overseas for extended periods of time are highly suspect, and upon coming back to the country must prove themselves true, in some cases, with exaggerated expressions of their Japaneseness: industriousness, self-effacement, and the observance of behavioral and interpersonal niceties. Meanwhile, foreigners, regularly checked and fingerprinted, have great difficulty acquiring Japanese citizenship.

Marginality is easy to come by and hard to lose in Japan, and that hazard is a powerful disincentive to be in any way "different." Those so marked of course don't want their children to suffer the same stigma. While intellectuals and critics may look for the social climate to change so that their children can be more independent, the adults themselves will limit the risks of differentness to the maximum extent possible. What this means is that education is a force for reducing cultural variety—thereby patrolling the predictable conformity on which Japanese society depends.

JAPAN IS UNIQUE: THE *NIHONJINRON* PHENOMENON

Although individual Japanese incline toward conformity, the nation as a whole believes itself to be utterly unique; there is no other place in any way like Japan. Hence we have a kind of "national individualism." The insistence on Japan special and apart has deep historical and cultural underpinnings, beginning, as most tales of national identity do, with a creation myth. The Japanese version goes like this: Izanami and Izanagi, brother and sister deities, gave birth to the islands of Japan along with a number of other deities. Ninigi, the grandson of Amaterasu, one of these gods, descended to the islands bringing the Three Imperial Regalia, symbols of power and legitimacy. And Ninigi's descendants became the first emperors.

The story of heaven-created islands dropped into the sea, Japan's myth of origin, is like many others which contend that a people and place were set into the world by divine intervention and thus bear the qualities of godhood. Some places of myth, like Mount Olympus in Greece, were to be the abodes and playgrounds of gods and marvelous human beings. Other places, like the Judeo-Christian paradise, were to be the scene of divine creativity and the moral testing of god-created beings. Still others, like holy places in India, were sanctified by accident, when gods in battle dropped a trident or when the bodily parts of gods who were dismembered fell to earth.

Japan was presumed to be the locus of an eternal line of divine rulers, Ninigi's offspring, a line that persists to the present. Therefore, one of the elements of the sense of Japanese uniqueness is mytho-historical continuity, which is regarded as both means and end for the society as a whole.

The uniqueness of being Japanese, the fact that one cannot *become* Japanese (Japan was not created by immigrant gods), is part of ongoing scrutiny in Japan—the *nihonjinron*, or "what it means to be Japanese," debate. In 1985 the matter was institutionalized in the form of an

Institute of Japanology in Kyoto, where scholars, social commentators, and "cultural persons" (*bunkajin*) are able to muse on the Japanese character and its place in the modern world. Having engaged academic and media attention for over a hundred years, *nihonjinron* is really an attempt to define Japanese culture in the face of threatening contact from other societies—a conscious effort to "know who we are" so as not to be swallowed up by Western influences. Indeed, during the Meiji period, *nihonjinron* developed the urgent tone of national security issues. While a sense of Japanese uniqueness is still intrinsic to the concern, the tone today is slightly less intense, and sometimes seems only a narcissistic parlor game. Still, as Hidetoshi Kato points out, "There is the inclination to emphasize that the Japanese are 'unique' in developing *nihonjinron*."[3]

Japanese education reflects the need to maintain a special identity. Education, during the Meiji period, was developed in part to institutionalize and perpetuate Japanese cultural identity. Thus, the centrality of Japanese history and culture in the curriculum has to be tied to the rise of modern nationalism. But a more benign reading of the Meiji and Taisho (1912–1926) period curricula shows that the development and perpetuation of national identity were used to forestall cultural colonization by the West, not to create aggressive national aggrandizement.

The modern curriculum is seen to provide a unique experience for the Japanese child that cannot be duplicated, or substituted for, by education anywhere else in the world. What the overseas Japanese child learns that he has missed, upon returning to Japan, is not only more math, Japanese language, social studies, and science, but forms of behavior, sets of influences, and social manners—what one teacher called "*Japanese* common sense"—without which his competence and identity are deeply flawed. This "common sense" is a moral construct, and contains both ways of relating socially to others and a "physical common sense" learned in school.

JAPAN'S MORAL "COMMON SENSE"

Japanese common sense, taught along with Japanese history and culture, is most evident in what is called "moral education." In its current manifestation, a child studies behavior and relationships within the family and community. A 1983 official description of the elementary school course of study states:

Moral Education . . . is aimed at realizing a spirit of respect for human
dignity in the actual life of family, school and community, endeavoring
to create a culture that is rich in individuality and to develop a democratic
society and state, training Japanese to be capable of contributing to a peaceful
international society, and cultivating their morality as the foundation thereof.[4]

Thus, the distinction that Western societies make between "social"
and "personal" morality is rarely made in Japan: a moral dilemma
is almost always regarded as a social or interpersonal problem, not
one to which prescriptive or proscriptive abstractions can be applied.

Among the goals of the school syllabus are those which a Westerner
would recognize, such as "respect for another's freedom" and "acting
according to one's own beliefs." Then there are some that are very
Japanese: "it is desirable that, in the lower grades, one should learn
to bear hardship, and in the middle grades, to persist to the end
with patience, and in the upper grades, to be steadfast and accomplish
goals undaunted by obstacles or failures." Furthermore, "in the lower
grades, one should learn to listen to the opinions of others and admit
frankly one's own mistakes or faults, and to behave unselfishly, and
in the middle grades, to live a life of moderation, and in the upper
grades, to reflect always on one's words and behavior, to act with
prudence and to live an orderly life." Zeal, striving, and self-abnegation
are to be combined with cheerfulness and sensitivity to others—all
within the context of learning "to love one's hometown and to protect
the land, culture and traditions of the motherland, and . . . to be
aware of one's responsibility as a Japanese."[5]

These high-sounding desiderata are inculcated through very concrete stories and exempla, which are usually presented as cases of
social dilemmas. Human relationships and interdependencies form
the central focus of these tales. A conflict of loyalties, a case of
temptation to bad behavior, a story of strife in a family, are given
to the children as problems to contemplate. And through open discussion a solution or analysis is developed by the entire class. As in
other such instances, the solution is not valued unless it is generated
by the class itself—and unless it has unanimous support.

In other words, the real agenda of the morals class lies not only
in the content of texts, but in the means by which the class reaches
an understanding. This process, which is slow and delicate, is called
nemawashii, or "digging around the roots." Just as one doesn't try
to pull up a tree stump without accounting for all the roots, one
doesn't try to impose a perspective or solution on a group without

eliciting the (wholehearted) consent of each individual; even a single unloosened root can prevent the release of the tree stump. *Nemawashii* represents more than an example of Japanese pedagogy and social ritual. There is a strong value placed on agreement and harmony, on the unity of purpose, which is at the very core of Japanese morality and which is accordingly the central agenda of Japanese education. This, along with other cultural values, is what is learned in a Japanese school and what is seen as uniquely Japanese.

Sound Mind in Sound Body

Japanese schools and parents are also especially concerned about the child's physical development, which is integrated with other forms of learning far more than it is in Western school curricula. To be a good child in Japan is to be strong, and the means by which such strength is developed is self-testing—pushing oneself as hard as one can—and also the ritualized exercises of the school day.

Physical education involves both morning exercises done by the whole school at one time and the more specialized classes in gymnastics, swimming (many schools have their own pools), and team sports. Knowledge of the right way to do the group exercises is important. Children coming from non-Japanese schools feel shame for not knowing how to do them properly, and teachers and parents will soon enough help them to get things right. The exercises, like those beginning a business day, are regarded as a way to get children into an energetic and positive frame of mind, and to dispel extra energy. Exercise is not usually undertaken to develop athletes—there are few "jocks" in a Japanese school—but to learn how to push oneself and develop unity with others.

Japan Looks to the Future

Felt continuity with the gods and emperors of the past does not run counter to the Japanese preoccupation with planning for the future. Futurology is a game Japanese play too, but thanks to resource scarcity and an accompanying sense of risk and dependence, Japanese planners play the game with deadly seriousness. What they feel is the primary and most dependable resource, Japan's well-educated and hardworking population, is the focus of the most intense planning. And children, because they are the future, get top priority in the exercise.

Moreover, social consensus has restricted births to an average of less than two per family. This has also helped to channel attention to the future of valued offspring. Parents of course worry most about their own children. But the society at large also understands the clear relationship between the Japanese educational and occupational worlds. Hence the school must both equalize opportunity and sort by ability. This latter principle of meritocracy further ensures that parents, teachers, and society carefully attend to *each* child's development, to maximize his or her "merit" in the race for society's rewards. In Japan one cannot inherit position, and, at least ideally, one has no assured ascribed route to success. As in the United States, a meritocratic system and individual psychic anxiety go hand in hand.

Yet while the pressure on Japanese parents and teachers is especially intense, the child is shielded. His ability, character, and identity are, to the maximum extent possible, protected from the onslaughts of worry about the future. Things will be fine, the child is continually assured, if he learns to persevere, to possess sincerity, and to show good cheer—the lesson of the morals course. A corollary here is that in Japan eventual success is not assumed to depend on one's innate capacities but on virtuous characteristics one *can* develop. Hence potential is regarded in Japan as egalitarian—everyone has it, but some work harder to develop it than others. In the United States potential is usually thought to be a bottom-line capacity that varies from person to person and that cannot finally be exceeded—you can only "do *your* best." Our kind of individualism implies a finite and ultimately restrictive notion of capacity; Japanese "potential" is accessible to all, though it may never be fulfilled by even the most able.

How the Japanese child's potential is to be maximized is society's responsibility, not the individual's. For the past forty years, the means for getting the most out of life have been very tightly tied to the educational system, and how well the child does in the schoolroom is felt to be the most important determinant of Japan's place in the future.

2

MOTIVATION AND MORES

Cultural Prerequisites for Learning

Japanese mothers and fathers usually think that their children are good children: they meet parental social and behavioral expectations and they also do well in school. And because they do well by means of intense personal engagement, we must assume that external pressure is not the only force at work. To ask my son's question again, "What makes them such good children?" The idea of what a good child is of course varies greatly from culture to culture, but there are some notions that span all modern societies, and clearly one of them is academic success. (Other expectations, mostly social or behavioral, vary more widely. The French feel that a child who is *bien élevé* is one whose social graces and general behavior are flawless; such a child shows none of the obstreperousness or disobedience of the *enfant terrible*. Americans like spunky, independent children—as long as they don't get in the way of parental priorities. Americans also prefer the all-around, open, good-natured youngster to the intense, inner-directed, and contemplative child.)

In Japan, learning and performing at high levels are characteristics of the good child. But he achieves because of a source of motivation more important in parents' and teachers' minds than good grades and test scores—forms of visible, quantifiable academic success. These are important, of course. But much more important are the moral and behavioral attributes of the child as he learns and performs. So Westerners are wrong when they stereotype the Japanese child's success as the product of harsh parental pressure, or the child's assimilation of an unaccountable "Japanese propensity for hard work," or his subjugation to relentless schoolroom competition. Even more distorted is the American protectionist cry that the Japanese have made world dominance in test scores a "national security issue"—to best us in the learning war. In the martial environment of the trade war, propaganda produces caricatures while subtler questions of personal incentive and motivation are ignored. A real understanding of the psychocultural environment of learning must be based on a grasp of the factors that the Japanese themselves stress and value.

Even while Americans see competition and the drive for personal achievement as the most significant elements behind academic success, these are surprisingly absent, or at least differently conceived, in Japan. Part of a much broader cultural and psychological environment of learning, the incentive to perform well in the classroom has deep roots in indigenous Japanese conceptions of the child and in the human relationships that give meaning to the child's life. The factors that I want to examine here include the cultural values shared by teachers and parents, as well as some of the goals and means of child rearing that distinguish the Japanese child's environment from his American counterpart's. To begin, we must set aside yet another preconception. Because the superficial similarities between the material cultures are so striking, and because Japan meets and exceeds our most obvious measures of a "modern society," we easily assume that Japanese children are raised on "modern, Western" principles and that whatever differences may exist are a matter of degree, not kind. But off the coast of Asia, in Japan, we encounter a different route to modernity, and, indeed, material success is a happy and incidental result of a human system based on a quite different set of priorities and expectations.

The most important cultural difference, which also crucially affects any child's development, lies in the place given to human relationships and "interdependence." In Japan human relationships are both the means and ends in successful child-rearing, which is unequivocally the responsibility of the mother. *Accordingly, the central human relationship in Japanese culture is between mother and child.* Much more later on the Japanese mother, but here I merely want to lay out the premises that govern her attitude and behavior. For one thing, she feels that her child possesses the potential for great success. In her eyes, he is born with no innate ceiling on his ability, and, with proper encouragement, he will be motivated to perform at high levels of achievement. What provides that impetus is, first, the mother's effort and commitment, and then through her, the child's own engagement in his development. In short, success results from a child's relationship with a devoted mother, and that relationship is created through *amae*.

AMAE

Sadaharu Oh, the legendary home-run hitter, recently wrote in his memoirs that his relationship with his family and teacher provided what he needed to succeed. As he describes it, the relationship between love and success in Japan is a crucial one. Oh says that it is through being cared for, indulged, and nurtured that he was fired to work hard enough to overcome his weaknesses on the field and to devise, among other things, his own batting stance, so that time and again he broke his own records. He says: "*Amae* warms the heart but it also enables you to work twice as hard, to overcome the siren songs of laziness." In other words, the assurance of security and unconditional love is a source of high human motivation, at least in Japan.

But understood more precisely, what is *amae?* It is a Japanese psychological concept which has been made famous in the outside world by Takeo Doi in his book *The Anatomy of Dependence*. Doi defines *amae* as "the desire to be passively loved" or the expression of the wish to be dependent, to be taken care of unconditionally.[1] Doi draws many examples from his psychiatric practice, and thus gives life to the concept from his experience with pathologies of insufficiently expressed or gratified *amae*. But he also draws attention to the wide range of normal situations in which *amae* is an expected and valued aspect of relationships at all ages in Japan. Doi does not claim that this kind of dependency is unique to Japan, but rather that everyone, as he says, "even a puppy," has need for it.

The existence of *amae* is universal, but it is of course stressed differently in various cultural environments. Americans make efforts to reduce the dependency of a child, and it is not uncommon to hear the mother of a two-year-old say "You're a big boy; you can do it yourself." This is to shame him into independent behavior. A Japanese mother would not want that for a young child; she would want more dependence rather than less, and she would *not work at all* to reduce his need for her at age two. As Caudill and Weinstein note, an American mother looks at the newborn as a dependent baby whom she must train to separate from her; a Japanese mother sees a gap between herself and the baby that she must try to bridge by encouraging what we would call dependence.[2]

Two types of valued goals are supported by child-rearing concepts and practices related to *amae:* first, those that affect the child's relationship with his total social environment, which is for the child his principal source of incentive and satisfaction; and second, those that affect the child's academic performance within the specific social environment of the school. Even this simple distinction is artifical, for *all* human qualities valued in Japan involve the social environment and *everything* that a mother dreams of for her child is ultimately tied to human relationships.

Hence, what we might call purely "personal" performance is seen not only as evidence of individual ability and skill, but also as a means for securing one's place in the social environment, which in turn substantiates moral character and appropriateness to the milieu. Because all valued individual qualities have a "moral" weight in Japan, and because "morality" is ipso facto a social morality, enhancing one's skills nearly always helps to cement one's place in the world of relationships. In the United States individual skills and ability mark one's individual, not social or group, identity.

For the Japanese, the most highly valued qualities are those which make a child *ningen-rashii,* "human-like,"[3] and the most valued among the qualities is an ability to maintain harmony in human relationships. To perform well in school and other settings is important, but that is mostly regarded as a visible demonstration of a capacity to be a good (social) person. Americans, by contrast, tend to give much higher priority to individual skills and attributes, "independence" key among them, and to see one's interpersonal skills as more superficial—"social graces," a *means* rather than an *end.*

Westerners may even see social skills as antithetical to the expression of the "true self"; they may feel that politeness hides a person's feelings, that social harmony results from "insincere" behavior—a denial of a person's individual feelings. Accordingly, to engage in the behavior denoted by the verb *amaeru* ("to pursue nurturance and indulgence") might be regarded in the West as a form of immature and selfish individualism.

But the quest for nurturance is not a selfish act in Japan. When *amae* is translated as "passive love," as Doi has done, it may sound negative and self-indulgent: a person gets but does not give in a relationship. But *amae* means an active, even generous search for care: when you seek another's indulgence and allow him or her to care for you, you are actually *giving* to the other person. By allowing yourself to be nurtured, you confer value on the caretaker, giving that person an opportunity to display the valued skills of nurturance.

Of course, as Doi points out, there are inappropriate displays of *amaeru,* times when potential caretakers must reject those seeking indulgence. The ability of any person to care for another adequately is finite and should not be misspent, and the obligation implied in a parental or surrogate parental role is not taken on lightly. Traditionally, a teacher or superior will not indulge all petitioners for special care and will not take on all willing disciples. Because a petitioner knows that, if accepted, the relationship will be lifelong and involve deep obligations on both sides, the petitioner must prove that he is worthy.

To think about *amae* also means that we must look into the cultural meanings of *freedom* as understood in the United States and Japan. Here freedom is the freedom to choose—which implies a degree of personal isolation and autonomy. You should, ideally, choose on your own, apart from the concerns of others or their preferred choices for you. In Japan freedom is the freedom to be indulged, to do as one likes within the bounds of a permissive relationship. Other Japanese concepts of freedom do of course exist, especially since Western influence has pervaded the Asian culture. But our notion of freedom pushed to the extreme seems full of loneliness and pointless to a culture where human relationships are the major wellspring and end of the value system. *Amae* in contemporary Japan may no longer be the complete and explicitly reinforced source of meaning in life; to some extent it has been replaced by borrowed ideologies of a different sort of individualism, especially for young people before the responsibilities of marriage and family. But *amae* still represents a very important personal value.

One must understand *amae* if one wants to understand how American and Japanese ideas about childhood, personal development, and education differ. *Amae* confounds our usual notions about independence and social relationships. When a Japanese child has a kicking and screaming tantrum in a public place as his mother whips out an always-available sweet, or when an American teenager demands the keys to the family car, the meaning of each cannot be understood in terms of what a single individual does or of the burdensome obligations of superior–inferior relationships. Both of these might, even in the West, be seen as understandable manifestations of feeling that exhibit both a desire for separation and a recognition of normal dependence.

But American concepts of personal development from earliest childhood do stress separation and individuation, while the Japanese concept of *amae* comes down on the side of the permanence of human relationships, especially with one's mother, where indulgence can be freely given and received.

We might wonder here if the American ideal of the unfettered individual self can be achieved, given the child-rearing and teaching methods we have espoused. If we really believe that a "good child" is a self-motivated, autonomous person who can choose for himself from an early age, why do our homes and schools have no consistent child-rearing and teaching methods which might produce such a child? Seeing a child who is a genuine "loner," who hears the beat of a distant drummer, a teacher in an American school would probably feel that something is wrong, especially if the child is not achieving at high levels. So we must ask if the assumptions that in fact govern the average American school, along with the demands of learning and the potent pressure of social conformity, aren't antithetical to our cherished concept of "independence." It may be that the truly independent person is actually marginal to our, or any, society. As Thomas Rohlen has said, "Our individualism is an attempt to deny social structure itself."[4]

In both the United States and Japan, however, a certain mythic glow is conferred on the solitary person. Our Lone Rangers are matched in Japan by the legends of wandering masterless samurai. The difference is that we have tried to incorporate the myth into the way we raise our children, and the Japanese have not. In fact, of course, very little real similarity exists between an American school graduate (or for that matter, a dropout) and the masked man in the Wild West.

In sum, the good child, or *ii ko,* is differently conceived in the United States and Japan. We have developed an ideology of child development, which shifts slightly with each change in fashion in popular psychology but maintains a core of consistent values. Independence and individual self-expression have priority as overt values in our child rearing. And while the capacity to cooperate and work comes up in parent–teacher conferences, these are never seen to take precedence. Moreover, "working to the best of his/her ability" figures greatly in teachers' reports. Yet because ambivalence exists between the idea that one has innate abilities and the idea that one can infinitely improve oneself, or at least infinitely change the specific environment in which one tests one's abilities, doing one's best is hard to define. One avoids the uncomfortable assessment that a failing child *is* doing his best.

We instead unconsciously assume that there's better in the child somewhere, and if his performance is poor, we blame environmental factors (a broken family, illness, impoverishment) rather than motivation and effort, as do the Japanese. And while we value the development of a child's capacities to the fullest, we have no particular external standards by which these capacities are measured. Hence frustration may arise when an infinity of American possibility is presented. A child is taught that he can go to the moon or the White House, if he wants to. At the same time he is also told that he can only work to his own capacity, and that his potential is innate, not achieved. Faced with a double bind, the child is often left confused, if not completely thwarted.

Furthermore, Americans tend to value externally measurable or personal attributes, even while standards for performance are not universally agreed upon. They value less a child's capacity to develop successful relationships with others, because those relationships themselves are not seen as part of personal development. Our children are taught to be considerate of others and to cooperate, but the lessons are meant to give the child ways to get on in the world; the qualities taught are not ends in themselves. "Interpersonal intelligence," to use Howard Gardner's phrase,[5] is used to "psyche out" the others. One is sensitive to others in order to advance one's own personal agenda, not to build meaning for one's life based on a regard for other people.

But relationships, and membership in a group, are important priorities in a Japanese child's socialization. A mother is proud of a child who shows that he is dependent on her, but she also understands that this capacity will help him meet the expectations of the world outside the family. The distinction between *uchi* (inside, home) and *soto* (outside) is an important part of the socialization of a child. Every group to which the child will belong as he grows up will resemble the original *uchi* of the family to some degree, having its own denominators and expectations of membership.

Japanese child-rearing values emphasize both the child's personal characteristics and the means by which a child accomplishes his goals.

Let us examine some of the terms which are used to describe a good child. Most frequently cited are *otonashii* (mild, gentle), *sunao* (compliant, obedient, cooperative), *akarui* (bright-eyed), *genki* (active, spirited, energetic), *hakihaki* (brisk, prompt, clear), and *oriko* (obedient, smart). This first group of terms sets out goals for personal growth, attributes to be encouraged through appropriate socialization.

The second group includes terms that describe the means by which a child's development is advanced both personally and socially. These imply a psychological theory and the activity through which the cultural theory of child development is implemented. Among the terms are *gambaru* (to persist), *gaman suru* (to endure hardship), *hansei suru* (to reflect on one's weakness), *amaeru/amayakasu* (meaning to depend/ to indulge), *wakaraseru* (to get the child to understand) and *rikai saseru* (to get the child to understand logically). These terms encompass strategies to be used in mother–child relationships (mainly nurturant) and teacher–student relationships (mainly didactic) that are in some ways congruent with Western categories of development—here compartmentalized as cognitive, emotional, and behavioral development. But there remain markedly different conceptions about the proper training of children: notions loosely called "indulgence" and "patience," practiced to achieve ends we have inaccurately translated "obedience" and "submission."

The important point is that there is in Japan no conflict between the goals of self-fulfillment and the goals of social integration. The bridge between them lies in the socialization that occurs in the relationship between mother and child. This relationship of course embodies Japanese ideas of nurturance and indulgence and is also fully consistent with the standards applied by larger social units. A mother is expected to recognize and be sensitive to her child's individual personality and inclinations; and yet, the characterization by or encouragement of idiosyncratic traits is not part of a mother's agenda. Knowing that your son is self-willed means that you know what strategy you must use with him to get him to cooperate; it does not mean that you reinforce or value the quality in itself.

Because a line cannot easily be drawn between social and personal, all this may appear more than a bit confusing to an American or Englishman. But the bottom line is a wide integration of self and society. This permits a highly nurturant indulgence in the mother–child relationship that is not only congruent with social discipline and order but actually contributes to it.

Let us look now at the word *sunao,* frequently translated as "obedient." It would be more appropriate to approach its usage through a cluster of meanings attached to it by Japanese mothers and teachers: "open-minded," "nonresistant," "truthful," or, as Kumagai says, "authentic in intent and cooperative in spirit."[6]

It is very hard to catch the nuances in English: naiveté, naturalness, simplicity, mildness, gentleness, and straightforwardness are part of the meaning. One Japanese mother said: "It means obedient if I see my child as bad; it means autonomous if he is good." She also noted that most mothers see their children as naturally good, needing only proper care to grow up "straight." Kumagai, meanwhile, points out that the English translation "obedience" implies subordination and lack of self-determination, but asserts that *sunao* "assumes cooperation to be an act of affirmation of the self."[7]

A child who is *sunao* has not sacrificed his personal autonomy on the altar of cooperation. Cooperating with others does not imply giving up the self, as it may in the West, but in fact implies that working with others is the appropriate means by which one expresses and enhances oneself. Engagement and harmony with others is a positively valued goal, and the bridge to open-hearted cooperation is sensitivity, as first understood by the mother's example and encouragement.

Another term, related to *sunao,* is, by its seemingly contradictory nature, equally difficult to translate and understand given the assumptions of Western child-rearing. This is *yutaka,* meaning "empathic," "receptive," or "open-hearted." Again, first appearances are deceiving. *Yutaka* has a very positive, active connotation and implies a mature vigor. "Sensitivity" and "anticipation of the needs of others" may sound passive and feminine to Western ears, but *yutaka* is hearty and confident, and implies receiving and giving in abundance, enjoyment of life within a social group, and caring for others' needs. Other translations include "having common sense in one's dealing with others" and "being fertile and abundant," as in a full-breasted, nursing mother. *Yutaka* has also recently appeared in official recommendations for educational reform. The hope is that by liberalizing education while maintaining the importance of traditional social morality, Japan can produce children with *yutaka na kokoro* (confident, sensitive hearts). Like *sunao,* both mother and school should encourage the development of *yutaka.*

How one raises a *sunao* child with a *yutaka na kokoro* who can also engage himself in tests of endurance and effort involves the technique of *wakaraseru* (getting the child to understand). In the process of *wakaraseru,* or engaging the child in the goals of his mother, the chief principle seems to be *never go against the child.* Where an American might see manipulation of the child through "indulgence" as preventing him from having a strong will of his own, the Japanese mother sees long-term benefits of self-motivated cooperation from keeping the child happy and engaged.

How, a Western observer may ask, can the use of indulgence to raise a child produce in the same child a commitment to disciplined effort? Again, there is no contradiction between "indulgence" and "effort." Taniuchi says intimacy and supportive attention to a child are used by the mother to teach him not only social standards but also the need to work hard to achieve and be valued in society.[8] "Love-oriented" techniques rather than "power-assertive" methods to discipline children are also cited in Conroy, Hess, Azuma, and Kashiwagi.[9]

The Western belief that sparing the rod spoils the child obviously assumes that discipline is good for the child in the long run, and not just for the immediate correction of a misdeed or fault. But "I'm only doing this because I love you" and "It hurts me more than it hurts you" need not be said in indulgent Japan. There is, however, a notion that a child benefits from experiencing hardship. *Kuro saseta hoo ga ii,* "It's better to have (the child) endure difficulties," is a very common expression. *Kuro* (suffering or hardship) is believed to have a beneficial effect on the self, deepening and maturing it, removing self-centeredness. Without *kuro* a person cannot be said to have grown up.

Japanese child-rearing manuals of the early eighteenth century[10] strongly advise parents to be strict with their children, to submit them to discipline. These manuals do not reflect contemporary practices, but because of the many warnings they contain against indulgence at home, we can infer that even then, mother and the home may have provided a "softer" environment for child rearing than educators believed healthy. The idea of requisite discipline is especially strong among the prewar and wartime generations, whose formative years were characterized by struggle and scarcity. According to many older people, contemporary mothers "overprotect" their children. In the eyes of older people, *kuro* still figures in child-rearing ideology.

Kuro can be psychological, physical, or environmental, and although small children are protected from it, the *kuro* of intensive study, or the wholehearted application of one's energies at the expense of pleasures, is said to be good for the older child. The example of Ninomiya Sontoku, the philosopher whose difficult childhood will be described later, was invoked to earlier generations of schoolchildren, and still exists, in the form of statues in school yards and stories in textbooks. Ninomiya embodies the virtue of hardship. Hardship builds character, which is not innate, and anyone, the Japanese believe, can acquire the habit and virtue of self-discipline.

THE PATH OF PURE ENDEAVOR

Suffering is not, itself, the point. Enduring is perhaps more important. The term *gambaru* (to persist) is frequently invoked by mothers, teachers, and peers. As Singleton points out,[11] teachers invariably tell parents that "it would be good if the child would just *gambaru* a little more" (*Moo sukoshi gambaru hoo ga ii to omoimasu*). Japanese persistence, which Western observers think is central to the Japanese personality, is not, as we might have it, the product of narrow vision, masochism, or lack of individual free will. The difference between Western and Japanese concepts of effort and personal commitment needs to be understood if we want to explain how our respective children's goals and performances vary. Why, in short, is Johnny told to "do his best," whereas Taroo is exhorted to "keep on struggling" even after he has bested his own best previous efforts? In Japan pushing on, persisting, not giving up, are in themselves important, and show once again the significance of the way something is done as more important than the end accomplishment.

In short, *gambaru* and *kuro* are aspects of self-discipline, which does not mean in Japan what it does in the West. As Ruth Benedict pointed out,[12] discipline is a culturally determined term, and while Westerners perceive discipline (like obedience) as necessary but potentially self-negating, Japanese see fully engaged discipline as refining and enhancing the self.

For us, individualism is based on the idea of individual free choice, and the "free" is more important than the commitment to a "choice." The idea of compelling oneself to struggle on, to delay gratification, and, in the end, to endure for endurance's sake seems to many Westerners to be a pointless sacrifice. But Japanese do not experience it this way, nor do they experience committed struggle as lonely. One *never* needs to endure alone.

As Morsbach says, the noncritical submission of the disciple to years of apprenticeship in Japan should not be seen as evidence of

> moral masochism . . . but rather as a part of reciprocal exchange. . . .
> The arrangement benefits both parties; and if the pupil endures long enough
> there is a good chance of being independent one day, or even paternally-
> dominant in turn in relation to his or her pupils. Meanwhile, the teacher
> has little fear of finally being upstaged: on the contrary, with increasing
> age prestige is likely to increase through the number and accomplishments
> of one's *deshi*. The latter, in turn, feel honour-bound to see that their
> *sensei* gets the official credit, even if it is common knowledge that this is
> no longer the real situation.[13]

One's health is an important factor in all this. Morsbach notes that "it is a commonly held belief that the body is greatly malleable as long as the will is strong."[14] Since the body will be subjected to trials, however, mothers and teachers consider health and accompanying physical strength as critically important to the child's ability to endure. In short, adults feel responsible for the child's physical well-being. Thus children are fed well, exhorted to exercise, and encouraged to test the limits of their bodies. One sixth-grader in Tokyo writes of her days in elementary school: "Above all, I became physically strong. . . . During the third grade, I tried to wear a short-sleeved shirt just like my friends in the winter. It was cold but I endured it. I did the same during my fourth and fifth grades. Then I realized I was becoming much healthier."[15] Teachers and parents worry that today's children are pampered, and that because of the stress on study, older children, especially, are weak.

The famous exhortation "Pass with Four, Fail with Five" means that if one is so lax as to sleep five hours rather than four, one will fail in the exams. Going without sleep is not seen (over a short period of time, anyway) as a problem: one can "crash" after the ordeal. In fact, many companies have rest houses in the country or contracts with seaside or hot-spring spas where their employees can unwind after an especially arduous spate of work. Like all sensible people, the Japanese understand that pressure and tension wreak havoc with the physical system. But neither can be avoided, and if healthy the body is seen to be able to endure and recover.

At least the *Japanese* body is so regarded. When Westerners entered a Zen temple in Kyoto and found the entrance requirements of silent, kneeling meditation for forty-eight hours too difficult, the temple created a double standard: Japanese must meditate for forty-eight hours, while Westerners can start with twenty-four.[16]

Meanwhile, mothers indulge infants and small children, and leave no bodily comfort unattended. They also continue to nurture older ones by their constant attention, expecting very little physical effort or exertion from them at home. Mothers do exhort *teachers* to push their children harder, and children are strongly affected by their peers in sports and other forms of academic endurance. The exhortation *Gambatte* (Push on! Persevere!) is constantly heard from classmates and teachers, and one's capacity to keep going is more important than winning or losing in the end.

Persistence is part of *seishin* (individual spirit and character development): what Singleton calls "the real content of any educational process."[17] All can participate and derive moral benefit, and those in less than ideal circumstances can find themselves a challenge that can build character.

Another form of Japanese self-discipline, encouraged in school and throughout life, is *hansei* (self-examination and reflection). This is both personal and social. A child is encouraged to practice such examination and to seek out his own sources of weakness, self-discovery being much better than having others point out flaws in character. Indeed, the cultural avoidance of criticism of others makes *hansei* all the more important. When an entire class engages in *hansei* together, the class examines its interactions, goals, and methods, and then develops a plan of action for changing things. *Hansei,* in short, is oriented toward improvement.

In *hansei,* as in other modes of active socialization, engagement is regarded as akin to success. Again, the development of valued qualities and skills in the child encompasses his active participation and wholehearted commitment to the goals shared by parents and teachers. Engagement is manifested by the style, tone, and mode that one takes into the performance of a task. Some Japanese words speak to the marriage of commitment, style, and action. *Hakihaki* includes an interesting cluster of desired qualities: brisk, active, quick, and clear. It also suggests that the child speaks forthrightly; the term is usually used positively to describe boys, or a little negatively for girls. *Tekipaki* (brisk and positive) and *kichinto* (accurate and punctilious) describe a child (or adult) who is also confident, upbeat, and cheerful. *Hakihaki*, when translated as simply "brisk" or "active," seems to a Westerner to imply the superficial and fails to convey the Japanese sense either of the engagement of the child or of the more than superficial significance attached to his style of performance.

WHAT IS A GOOD MOTHER?

How is all the youngster's affective engagement, as well as the incentive to achieve and to conform to external expectations, encouraged within the primary "indulgent" relationship of mother and child? Let us begin to answer this question by noting that Japanese mothers are said to be "the best Jewish mothers in the world."[18] Like "Jewish mothers" everywhere, Japanese mothers feel that they are responsible for their children's future. And this belief, coupled with the importance of the child's success for the mother's own identity, is the basic source of a child's success in school—and, as some Japanese observers insist, the source of his problems as well.

But what it means specifically to be a good mother differs greatly from culture to culture. The good mother in middle and upper middle class America has a task-oriented concept of her role. This has produced the caricature of the "supermom": a woman who can list a positively inhuman number of successfully completed tasks and still appear fresh and appealing at the door when her husband returns. The Japanese mother does not feel the need to perform so many discrete tasks, no need for "notches on her belt." And she certainly would not see any part of her role as that of temptress and lover. For her, constant nurturant attention to her child, plus a home-cooked meal for her late-arriving husband, will suffice unto the day.

Accordingly, the expression "just a housewife" in no way conveys a Japanese mother's sense of her life and role. Her work, whether loving preparation of an artfully composed and nutritious lunchbox or thorough immersion in her child's math lesson, is seen to demand the best of her. There are few Japanese mothers drumming fingers waiting for their youngest child to enter full-time school so that they can get back into a career a Western woman might need to feel productive and important.

The phrase expressing the traditional ideal of Japanese womanhood, "a good wife and wise mother" (*ryosai kenbo*), still carries great meaning today, with the emphasis now on the "wise mother." Other forms of work and self-expression, and indeed, even the enhancement of the marital bond itself, are not regarded as highly as being a good mother. The family, a woman's source of influence and value, is embodied in the vertical ties of parent and child, rather than in the Western nexus of husband and wife. This Confucian-based ideal is strongly supported by Japanese women themselves, 76 percent of whom in recent polls say that their first responsibility is to their children.

Moreover, work of any kind in Japan is regarded as requiring absolute 100 percent effort, and a person who tries to combine different work lives is seen as confused and perhaps suspect, or at least lacking a fixed group identity. This is as true for men as for women. Few men are part-time workers or change companies without facing damaging consequences. A Japanese person is valued by the degree of commitment he invests in an activity, and more, by the degree of engagement he has in the human relationships that give meaning to that activity. Often the measure of the engagement is the amount of face-to-face time spent on the job, which is to say, within a work relationship. So it becomes obvious that a mother who works outside the home can give the necessary 100 percent nowhere.

An American observer of Japanese mothers might accuse them of excessive emotional investment in their children. What we call "mom-ism," however, is not what happens in Japan, and even a caricature of a Japanese mother in no way resembles a Mrs. Portnoy. The latter ties her children to her apron strings, nagging and controlling them through guilt and other forms of negative manipulation. She is finally empty without her children, confused about herself and her relationship with other adults.

Except for pathological cases, Japanese moms do not mistake themselves for their children, and what we may see as dangerous "merging" is a socially valued engagement in empathy and nurturance. There are of course complaints in Japan, especially among educators and in the media, against the extremes of bad mothering. These are represented by the "overprotected" child, who can do nothing for himself, and by the "latchkey" child, who wears his house key around his neck and comes home to an empty kitchen. There is a campaign against both. The mother who overprotects is seen to be "selfish," in a particularly Japanese sense of the word. Her selfishness is not individualistic, but rather the selfishness of the she-wolf who protects her cubs and completely ignores the society beyond. She cares only for the welfare of her own child and the environment of her own home. The working mother of a latchkey child is the focus of even more attention, for she is, in Japanese eyes, un-nurturant. I once participated on a panel in Tokyo whose subject was the lives of working mothers. At an afternoon session, a television news team took notes and filmed our discussion. I watched the broadcast of our session later that evening and found to my horror that my remarks had been significantly altered. To suit the expectations of the audience, the statement I had made about Japanese attitudes toward working women and the effect the attitudes might have on children was changed. I was made to say something I did not—namely, children who return home to an empty house after school will suffer in various ways. All this was accompanied by a very graphic set of drawings.

The first showed an empty kitchen, with a child sitting at a table, and the clock showing 4:00 p.m. With tears running down his cheeks, he held a school report card with "failure" written on it. The next drawing showed a kitchen with a happy child sitting at a table, a snack in front of him, displaying a splendid set of grades to his apron-bedecked, attentive mother. The producers of the show had crafted the standard message, knowing how the audience would respond in advance, and ignored the more complex (and far less dramatic) picture I had tried to create.

The fact is, however, that Japanese mothers who work outside the home do have great difficulty finding adequate care for their children. Daycare for infants and toddlers is rarely available, except as found by mothers who absolutely have to work. Most try first to put the child with a grandmother or other kin. And that most popular way of earning money among American teenagers, babysitting, has at least two strikes against it: the high schooler's preoccupation with study and the mother's preoccupation with her job of mothering.

But mothers everywhere, of course, gain value and satisfaction from the success of their children. Japanese mothers represent an extreme. When does the intense emotional investment begin?

It starts during pregnancy, when the mother is already seen to be responsible for the child's future health and intelligence. A young woman I know, pregnant for the first time in the United States while her husband was studying at an American university, was bombarded by her Japanese kin with advice, lore, and material supplies. Most came from her own mother and aunts, and this was altogether at odds with what she got from her American obstetrician and friends. The Japanese advice included admonitions to stay at home as much as possible, to bind her belly with tight sashes, to eat no eggplant and other tabooed foods, to read only uplifting, positive books, and to wear socks *always*. This was meant to engender the fetus's well-being. The American advice regarded maternal health as at least as important as fetal development, and in no case asserted that what the mother did would affect the child's future mental, psychological, and characterological development.

Taikyo, or "education in the womb," is something with a long tradition in Japan, and implies positive cognitive, moral, and general developmental intervention before birth. As with certain traditions in the West, the mother's womb is thought to be an ideal environment for the fetus, and leaving it is believed to be traumatic. Thus the recent popularity in Japan of a recording of "the sounds of the womb," which, it was thought, would benefit every Japanese newborn as he adjusted to the world outside.

Early Mothering

Once the baby is born, the mother's tasks begin in earnest. First, the baby is seen to be born with no particular abilities or disabilities, and the efforts of *taikyo* are seen at best to contribute to the creation of a blank slate, a tabula rasa. The practices of *taikyo* are mostly designed to prevent harm to the child's potential, rather than to enrich or lend advantage to the child. The mother's role after birth as well in providing an appropriate environment and stimuli is crucial: she must provide all that is needed to establish the child in society—up to and throughout schooling.

What sort of environment does the mother want to create? The first and most important element in it is herself, and her constant availability. Japanese mothers are almost always with their babies, and are physically close to them much more of the time than are American mothers. The Japanese mother sleeps and bathes with her child, and holds him or carries him next to her constantly. A Japanese phenomenon, which they call "skinship," is the closeness one experiences by touching, preferably skin to skin. And this is what the mother provides. Babies, not left in cribs or playpens, are always taken with the mother rather than left with babysitters or kin when she does errands or goes visiting. Moreover, Japanese babies are not put in carriages or strollers, but are carried strapped on the mother's back. While in the past older siblings might care for younger ones, these older children are now too busy with studies, or are not seen as appropriate caretakers by the contemporary mother. Meanwhile, the father, even on family excursions, is rarely seen with a baby on his back because this would show that he had taken a maternal role. But he might take a turn and rather awkwardly carry an infant in his arms if the mother must tend to an older toddler or carry purchases.

The mother customarily sleeps beside her infant, either lying next to the child's *futon* or placing the baby on her own. This makes nursing easier. A mother justifies the practice by saying she can keep the baby from disturbing other members of the household. But sleeping near others is traditional practice in Japan; even in homes in which each child might easily have his own room, children sleep together or with adults. When I once helped a Japanese graduate student find housing for his family in Boston, we visited several apartments. Because he and his wife had a new baby, I suggested that an apartment with a second bedroom would be perfect. The father, surprised and confused, asked me to repeat this unlikely suggestion, to which he finally replied, ''The baby sleeps with us, of course: he'd be lonely without us—that room will be my study.''

Besides the mother's availability and intimacy, what else does she offer to the child? In studies that compare mothering in the United States and Japan, researchers have shown that American mothers spend less time just being with the child in the same room. Also American mothers talk with their infants more than do Japanese mothers, who spend most of their time in close proximity to the child but say less and vocalize only when trying to lull the child to sleep. They also do not as often try to elicit a spoken response from the child.

American mothers will busily go in and out of a baby's room, neatening up, doing things perhaps unrelated to the specific care of the child. A Japanese mother will sit quietly by the side of the baby, or even lie down beside a napping infant. The American mother might rub the baby's back until he falls asleep, or sing to him, but will stop when he falls asleep. A Japanese mother will continue to pat the baby, rock him, or carry him long after he has drifted off. One could say that the American sees her role as a set of tasks, such as ''getting the baby to sleep,'' and the Japanese sees herself as ''being with the baby''—even ''merging with the baby.'' Sitting by the *futon* as he sleeps is thus not time wasted but part of her commitment to the relationship. For her, there is nothing more worthwhile that can be done.

Throughout, the Japanese mother's job is to prepare the child for life, to help provide a bridge between the home and the outside world. She gets to know the child, and then gradually exposes him to the norms of social and institutional settings. Constantly, she is alert to the norms of good mothering as reinforced by the *seken*— the community of neighbors, kin, teachers—all those who will measure her own and her child's qualities. The *seken* is not something to which you belong, like a family or school or workplace, but is rather a watchful normative presence, a "what will the neighbors say?" influence. All valued qualities, either personal or social, are important to the *seken,* and not just those that explicitly help to cement relationships. In the end, all such relationships are important to one's place in the social nexus.

Attending to a child's character and predilections, socializing him to the values of society while enhancing his specific skills, maintaining the proper profile of mothering in the *seken,* are time-consuming and result in a definition of mothering as a full-time job. How well the mother nurtures, in short, is measured by the *seken,* just as the *seken,* including teachers and examinations, measures her child. The mother's investment in her child, therefore, is an investment in the mother herself.

Concepts in Conflict: Differences Between Generations

Yoshie Uchida is a thirty-two-year-old housewife who has two children, ages nine and seven. The elder is a boy, Hiroshi, and the younger is a girl, Junko. The father is a white-collar employee of a large automobile manufacturer. The family lives in western Tokyo, near but not with the father's parents.

Yoshie graduated from a four-year college. She majored in child psychology and now reads widely, with a special interest in Western books on children and education. Dr. Spock, in translation, had a great effect on her, especially the emphasis on breastfeeding on demand. She resisted pressure to bottle-feed her babies, even while her mother-in-law constantly worried that the mother wasn't providing enough milk. Also concerned about the children's toys, Yoshie joined a group of mothers who did some modest research on toy safety. But aside from an intellectual bent toward child rearing, Yoshie is an "ordinary" young Japanese mother.

Her mother-in-law has been suspicious of her practices from the beginning. Among other things, Yoshie bought a Sears baby crib, nearly unheard of in her mother's generation and rarely used even by younger women. The crib was the subject of much family controversy. The mother-in-law said that the baby would be lonely sleeping away from the mother and would sleep less well because the mother couldn't lie down beside it to lull it to sleep. The mother-in-law also asserted that the crib was ugly and looked like a zoo cage.

The problem now is Yoshie's permissive attitude toward study. Yoshie feels that the children will be forced to work hard soon enough and she'd like them to have a "happy childhood." Yoshie has also not helped the children with homework, but does look over their papers and workbooks late at night. In partial concession to the mother-in-law, she has enrolled the children in *juku,* after-school classes where the boy learns English (not required at school) and the girl studies piano. The mother-in-law grumbles but allows that the children are at least learning to discipline their efforts through such classes.

The mother-in-law also does not like the fact that the children have no responsibilities for housework or other tasks around the home. She says they will grow up to be weak and dependent if they don't know how to take care of themselves. But when she found Yoshie teaching the boy to sew, she was appalled.

To some degree, Yoshie has been supported by her husband, but she herself has begun to wonder if she's doing the right thing. After all, the children will have to endure difficult trials later for which she should prepare them. And, because her mother-in-law tells her that other women in the neighborhood have criticized her, her zeal for Western child-rearing has weakened.

Yoshie's attitudes toward her children's upbringing are most clearly seen as "Japanese" if contrasted to opinion found in the United States. In a 1981 survey (see the figure on page 40) the following "characteristics of the good child" were examined by Japanese and American mothers (*J* and *U* in the figure), who were then asked which they would select as the three most important out of the list.

As can be seen from the figure, Yoshie and other Japanese mothers prefer children whose habits are regular, who avoid causing trouble for others, and who persevere. American mothers say they prefer independence, initiative, and tolerance. Nobody can say whether the mothers get what they want, but we can say that Japanese children are reasonably well socialized in the desired qualities; American children may be encouraged to be "independent," but in the long run,

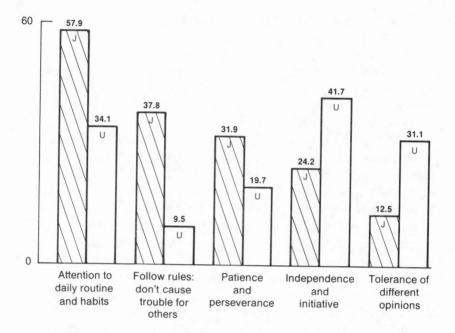

exhibit conformity to social norms. At least in those American schools where diversity is most evident, tolerance for others' differentness is not especially common.

WILL MOTHERING CHANGE?

Catherine Colman, an American family therapist practicing in Kyoto, has noted some changes among Japanese mothers, especially among the women who live in large urban apartment complexes. These women are isolated for most of the day. Even though her clients represent pathologies and not the norm of behavior and response, Colman still wonders if a crisis might be in the offing for Japanese women. Because virtually all of them marry and have children, and because most do not work nor are otherwise engaged outside the home, she is worried that isolation will produce even more intensely dedicated mothers—mothers who will soon enough experience what Western mothers know as the "empty nest syndrome." Or will the young women who are today considering careers instead of just "before marriage jobs" turn their backs on nurturance, which has been so highly valued in Japanese society? Colman in the end feels that Japanese women, like Japanese society, can continue to change without denying basic cultural values. Japanese women will undoubtedly go on for some time to choose the demanding and satisfying role of mother.

MOTHERING AND LIGATURES

An American mother sees her newborn as a dependent being who must be trained to become independent. A Japanese mother sees her baby as a being who, having separated from her and become independent, needs to learn how to become dependent upon her once again. This basic difference in attitude explains why child-rearing practices are so different in Japan and America, and also why the definitions of a women's roles stand in stark contrast.

The American mother wants to see her child develop as a fully separate person, prepared to discern and select among choices life will offer, to maintain the value placed on the concept of "freedom." The Japanese mother wants to cement a bond, to merge with the child, to raise him prepared for other interpersonal linkages in life. Besides the welfare of her child, the American mother must also constantly protect her own independence, her own freedom to choose, and thus she builds independence in her child to protect herself as well. The Japanese mother needs the validating bonds, and thus, to protect her own identity, works to reinforce a dependent relationship with her child. This is not only a model for other relationships which he will develop, but is the stuff of life itself for both mother and child.

Besides the cognitive development of her child, the Japanese mother attends to his social and psychological development. Cooperation, mutuality, and sensitivity to others rank high on the list of desired social characteristics of children but cannot be taught explicitly within the intensity of the mother–child relationship as it exists in modern urban Japan. While extended families, or nuclear families with large numbers of children, traditionally provided a natural arena for learning to cooperate and share, children today have little opportunity to interact in this way within the family. The average number of children in a Japanese family is just under two, and the omnipresence and attentiveness of the mother prevents even siblings from learning valued social skills by trial and error. A mother tends to intervene and orchestrate relationships between children; at the playground or other public places, she feels hesitant about her child's interactions with non-kin, since bad behavior will reflect on her, and she cannot admonish or reprimand a child not her own. Cooperation that used to be taught in the family is now taught later, in school.

GETTING AHEAD AND WORKING TOGETHER: THE VALUES OF THE GROUP AND SCHOOL

The closeness of mother and child remains protected, even as the child moves into widening circles of affiliation. That closeness provides the child with the motivation to work well in the classroom, and eventually to form deeper ties in work teams.

The mother's "good child" and the congruent notions of the primary school classroom persist in the later years of schooling but are displaced a bit by the "tougher" road of personal effort and more deliberate group organization. "Persistence" and "hardship" come to flavor the advice of elders more strongly, while peer pressure molds the child into behavior acceptable to the community.

While one's behavior is monitored to fit the criteria of acceptability in the group, there is a complementary and comforting relaxation of a child's direct responsibility for individual success and failure. He learns that cooperation may mean self-restraint and accommodation to the views of others, but he also learns that personal rewards exist in deep mutuality, and that success in simply working well within a team is itself highly valued. It is not just that "getting ahead" depends on the backing of a wide network of affiliates: the security, support, and affiliation in themselves are personal goals. Those who don't have a strong group affiliation are seen as poignantly, pathetically lonely—or as suspiciously independent.

There is of course a deeper sense of mutuality in a Japanese group than in an American group or organization, where affiliation seems—paradoxically, if you are Japanese—to depend on the self-interest of individuals. The American group defines itself rather loosely, to accommodate a person's needs to maintain his own mobility and to develop individuated skills and career paths. Thus absences for various reasons (family illness, the birth of a child, self-improvement in training courses, vacations) are legitimate and do not greatly hamper a person's ability to reintegrate on return. Membership depends on a vaguely-defined and rather abstract and contractual set of criteria—

based on choice, convenience, and specialization—rather than on a commitment to the active maintenance of the concrete set of relationships that make up the group. The degree of cohesion maintained is just enough to work toward the goals of the group; cohesion is not itself a goal.

The Japanese group accomplishes its goal as a whole, with less emphasis on specialized skills and more on a coordinated commitment of effort by everyone. Hence the respect and sensitivity people show each other are not seen as repression of the individual's will, but as generating direct and positive input into relationships through which the most meaningful individual benefits result. Furthermore, people who can deeply engage together in mutually reinforcing persistence are, by strongly held cultural conviction, good people.

In school, as well as at the workplace, the desirable qualities are those that reinforce team membership as well as those that are directly pertinent to the work itself. To consider the latter is not to diminish the former: a person's membership is enhanced by his performance on the job. In Japan an occasion is put together just so a group can be together and socialize. A college ski club, for example, will meet throughout the summer at the beach, coffee shop, or jazz club.

THE SKILLS THAT COUNT

The Japanese do, of course, value personal and individual skills, apart from those that contribute to group solidarity. What are those that count? Some may be obvious, like diligence or "stick-to-it-iveness," but others, like "sincerity" and "intuition," need further exploration. Among those highly valued by Japanese parents and teachers:

1. *Learning to gather and use large amounts of information.* This comes to bear, in the later years of schooling, on the examinations for entrance into high school and college. But a child's memory is trained early, and even a small child is encouraged to learn by rote long poems and songs. Meanwhile, adults have a repertory of performance pieces which they can call upon at *karaoke* bars, during which Americans, embarrassed and faltering, can't quite remember all of "America the Beautiful." Japanese children engage in fact cramming in the later years of secondary school, but it is less well known that they are explicitly taught learning strategies for sorting and organizing

knowledge. In other words, they are taught to discern or create relevant key categories for ordering information, and, rather than seeing facts as isolated bits of data, they are taught to work through the relationships between the facts.

2. *Learning to work diligently and in an organized manner.* Although part of the concern with categorization, this is more directly associated with concrete work habits. The *process* of work is emphasized as much as the end result, and the details of the method are stressed. Diligence means seeing the job through to the end, sticking attentively to a valued procedure, not cutting corners. Schoolwork must be finished, impeccably. Well-done assignments are *teinei* (correct) and *kirei* (beautiful and clean).

3. *Learning to do things with sincerity* (seijitsu), *also translated as "wholeheartedness" or "single-mindedness."* This form of dedication is close to diligence but implies a moral commitment to work, not just a nose-to-the-grindstone, forced march through a series of tasks. You must give yourself to the job, but, as in a good love relationship, you don't give your *self* away by doing so. You gain in exchange what is called an *ikigai,* or "reason for being." Every job is, ideally, seen as a complete life for a person who gives 100 percent. The dedication demands that a person invest his energies in one place only. People who have two jobs have two different group memberships, which makes their loyalties and commitment ambiguous or suspect.

4. *Learning to be a "quick study."* Dr. Shigefumi Nagano calls this the "potential for multiple aims," allowing a person to grasp a key problem in a new area and bring relevant material to bear upon it.[19] This is particularly important in Japan, where key employees are nonspecialists and elite job designations are generalist. Specialist jobs are usually lower in status. Thus an important skill is the ability to shift from one task to another—to be both jack and master of all trades (*kusai-yakyu*). Some have called this a "catch-up" form of competence, claiming that Japanese industrialization and technological development have depended on the quick grasp and deft application of both material knowledge and abstract concepts.

5. *Learning to develop* kan, *or a "grasp."* Kan, a useful tool in "quick study," encompasses a range of cognitive attributes, including:

Intuition, or a "sixth sense"
Premonition
A natural knack for doing things
Inspiration
A fast realization of what is needed for a task

Kan is considered essential in traditional skills and techniques, such as the plastic arts and crafts, and in self-defense. *Kan* is also a "sixth sense" in social relationships: you need to anticipate what others will think and feel, to understand what will help and harm a relationship, and what is needed to preserve a comfortable environment in the group. Thus you consciously manipulate the social environment, which is necessary to your own development, but do not damage the harmony of human relationships in the process.

The above-mentioned qualities are both explicitly and implicitly valued in schools. In the list of objectives presented to teachers of moral education classes, the following are emphasized, in the order given:

1. Diligence
2. Endurance
3. Ability to decide to do the hard thing
4. Wholehearted dedication
5. Cooperativeness

The only explicitly *group*-oriented objective comes last in the list. This doesn't mean that priority is given to individual development; in fact, the Japanese group assumes that its members will cooperate and be nurtured within it. Thus a child's attention to personal diligence, endurance, and other virtues is also assumed to be dedicated to the greater good of the group.

The Growth of a Counter-Image: What Is "Cool" in Japan?

The five virtues listed above are valued in the good child (*ii ko*) by parents, teachers, and the Japanese child himself. But, like children everywhere, the Japanese youngsters have a counter-image of the good child. In the rage of current concern about publicized incidents of *ijime,* or the bullying of children by their peers, we can see what it means to be popular, to be "cool." We can also see what problems a Japanese youth might experience trying to be all things to all people. Analyzing the causes of bullying, psychologists interviewed children in middle schools and asked for the characteristics of a child who gets bullied. These interviews and other case histories of children who have been tormented by their peers tell us what it means to be unpopular in Japan.[20]

First, unpopular children are *not* part of any group; they are alienated or have been rejected by cliques within the class. Some of these children attempt to gain acceptance by hanging around, visibly available to the others, or by being explicitly pushy (*deshabari*). Others withdraw. They may be excluded for many reasons, such as "being a nuisance" or "being slow," "being a messy, dirty person," "being a liar," "being two-faced." But the most common reason reported is that the outcast is "different."

Second, these children may exhibit qualities that produce jealousy or competition in the group, and chief here is *majime,* "seriousness." The child who is bullied may be a greasy grind, antisocial, and quiet. The quiet child was valued in the past, but now he is described as *ne ga kurai* (*nekura*), or "dark-spirited," not the lively, sociable, "bright-spirited" (*ne ga akarui* or *neaka*) child. The terms, particularly the abbreviated forms *neaka* and *nekura,* are part of common parlance today, thanks to their use (and possible invention) on a recent popular television show that made concrete the tendencies of "extroverts" and "introverts" and categorized them as "good" or "bad" types of children. Contemplation and quiet in children seem now to indicate sneakiness to their peers, even if the attributes are not associated with cramming and high grades.

The third outstanding characteristic of unpopular children is said to be a "victim mentality"—*higaisha-ishiki*—that provokes bullying. We will talk about bullying more later as a response to academic pressure in the schools and as a focus of attention for adult criticism of the educational system. Here it is only cited as evidence of a growing rift in the consensus about the good child.

As indicated by *neaka* and *nekura,* the media have engendered a new general vision of what children should be. On a currently popular television show, the host, Kinchan, introduces each week a *yoiko,* a *waruiko,* and a *futsunoko* (good, bad, and ordinary types of children). Now popular linguistic currency, the exaggerated caricatures of the television actors playing the three roles have become the embodiment, at least in shorthand, of value.

One kind of popular teenager is epitomized by the young, bouncy, pert pop star—a *burikko,* which means a child who pretends to be sweet and innocent. Sated by the saccharine, some teenagers have launched an anti-*burikko* movement. They say they don't like the "canned" characters of the young stars, and favor something more idiosyncratic, natural, and perhaps more sophisticated.

While children everywhere have always had a counterculture, and while even in Japan some distinction has always existed between the welfare of the group and the private needs of the individual, there is now overt tension between the ideals set for the child by adult society (and seen as required for future success) and those of the group with which the child spends most of his waking hours. An energetic, alert, bright-eyed youngster is of course valued by adults. But in the peer group, such energy is evidence more of "with-it-ness" in cool pursuits than conformity to adult goals, an alignment which can now become an overtly negative attribute. There are nerds even in Japan, a new distinction developing between a child who does well and a child who is "one of the gang." At the moment the distinction seems more important to the child at middle-school level, where considerable diversity still exists, than in high school, where academic streaming makes the goals of classmates more homogeneous. The crucial importance of the examinations is felt uniformly across the high school class, its members sharing an understanding of what it means to be a completely serious student.

THE MORALITY OF LEARNING AND WORK

Because learning in Japan is a moral activity, a school is regarded as a moral environment. So also is the workplace, where a person's virtue is tied to his performance. At the same time, buffering the moral wound of failure and shortcoming is the idea that everyone will be supported, that in Japanese society there is a place for everyone.

Accordingly, Japanese workaholism, however understood by the world outside, finally stems from an effort to demonstrate to others that one is a good person: in short, a happy by-product of a strenuous effort to develop a moral community. *Dantai ishiki,* or "organization consciousness," aims to create not only a commercial product, but also a deeper and surer sense of personal belonging. In the West an implied or explicit contract defines membership in a group and many other relationships: work for pay, possibility of promotion, marital rights, and conditions of financial support. The Japanese worker is part of a network of permanent, kin-like relationships characterized by mutual, long-term obligations and support. So what makes people exert themselves is the drive to perpetuate the supportive relationships that give value, continuity, and meaning to individual lives.

On a chilly city street in Japan during the winter, you will find people wearing white cotton masks over their noses and mouths. A Westerner would probably assume that they are trying to keep from getting colds or breathing polluted air. But the Japanese wear the masks when they themselves have colds, to prevent *others* from catching *their* colds. It is this sense of responsibility for others that pervades all Japanese social relationships.

Western public morality, meanwhile, is based on individual rights and individual self-realization. This presumes that a person will create his own social and economic relationships rather than inheriting them, that explicit contractual rules will characterize the relationships, and that an abstract legal system will enforce them. What is assumed to be permanent are the individual and the contract, not the social nexus. In Japan (and in much of the non-Western Asian world) morality is grounded on respect, duty, obligation, and responsibility within permanent reference groups that channel an individual's energies. A Japanese person is motivated to work hard because the group is *not* an amorphous mass in which his "selfhood" gets lost; rather, the group is a collection of active human mutualities that depend on individual contribution to provide the contributor with very personally experienced rewards.

Why don't the Japanese lean on their hoes? Why does Sadaharu Oh sweat to hit one more home run when security and nurturance already exist to the fullest? Now we can begin to understand. Collective action doesn't deny the role of an individual's skills and energies, and his personal contribution is fully noted. What motivates him to work so hard without an "individualized" reward is the promise— to use the language of social science—of a stable reference group and the predictable satisfaction it provides. Put another way, the Japanese did borrow the Western academic-occupational prestige hierarchy, with the attendant meritocratic-egalitarian access to the top. But they maintained the Japanese meaning of learning and performance and local values placed on social ties, seniority privileges, stability, and permanent loyalties.

The combination has led some observers to see Japan as a "mixed" culture, with feudal or pre-modern relics, holdovers giving a "Japanese flavor" to the most modern society in the world. But to see the family-like work relationship as an antique cultural artifact is to ignore its place as a healthy, vital source of human motivation in contemporary society. The reason why Japanese industry works and why Japanese schools teach, why workers don't quit and why children don't drop out of school, is that what is most wanted out of life—stability, security and support—are acquired through effort and commitment. This lesson is taught to the young, at home and at school.

3

JAPANESE SCHOOLS

Perspectives from History

Schools in Japan show evidence of many foreign influences and much change over time, but all the influences have undergone the alchemy of Japanization. What is most distinctively Japanese, aside from the evident culture of the school itself, is the consistency of concern for children: from daily care given by mothers, to the way the principal's office is run, to the planners at the ministry of education.

Of course, Japanese institutions and practices surrounding the care of children have changed over time, just as they have in the West. Earlier learning in Japan was primarily geared to buttressing traditional morality; later education became a matter of survival, and still later a political vehicle. But at all times the mode and outcome of schooling have been seen as critically important to the child and to society at large. Here I want to look at education during the past two hundred years, as it has reflected a tenacious consensus that Japanese society should be fully mobilized around and for children.

An interest in education for as many as possible greatly antedated the introduction of Western schools to Japan. Literacy, numeracy, and a moral education were considered important for people of all classes. By 1872, when Western models of universal schooling were introduced, Japanese literacy levels were already high: approximately 43 percent of boys and 15 percent of girls had been schooled and could read by the age of fifteen. Even in a society predominantly agrarian (only 20 percent of the population lived in urban areas), learning was clearly evident. While the pace and cycle of agricultural activities determined the actual attendance of children, enrollment rates in various types of school were, compared to European levels, fairly high.

LEARNING AND VIRTUE

Japanese cultural values and goals always supported the idea that a *good* person was one who studied, and that learning contributed to, as well as reflected, virtue. A model of scholarly goodness for Japanese children, from the Meiji period to the present, has been Ninomiya Sontoku, a Tokugawa-period philosopher whose statue still stands in many schoolyards. His legend was an especially powerful inspirational force during the Meiji period, when the efforts of the individual to rise were to contribute to the rapid modernization of Japan.

As an orphaned child, Ninomiya Sontoku lived with his uncle, a stingy and demanding man who made him spend long hours tilling ricefields. The child, however, yearned to study to improve himself, and, exhausted as he was, stayed up late at night to read Confucian texts. His uncle complained of the waste of lamp oil and so Ninomiya grew rapeseed in a small unused plot and pressed his own. A skilled farmer, he reclaimed wasteland to grow more crops and sold them to buy himself freedom from his uncle; he then returned to his father's land to work and study. Ninomiya's statue always shows him as a boy, carrying a heavy load of firewood on his back, bent over as he walks, reading a book.

What made Ninomiya the exemplar of Japanese nineteenth-century morality was his self-discipline, willingness to work hard, and drive to learn. In his legend study was associated with agricultural work, and was not seen as a way to rise above labor in the fields, but rather as a means by which a person of whatever occupation realized his best potential by improving his character and virtue. Here scholarly goodness was not divorced from manual labor as it was in traditional China.

In other Japanese Horatio Alger stories, hard work, as well as a strong communal consciousness not emphasized in the Ninomiya Sontoku legend, combined to produce both personal and social virtue. However, unlike the American Horatio Alger stories, the happy ending for the Japanese hero was in no way contingent on personal reward: harmony in interdependent relationships is both goal and setting for sufficient proof of one's virtue.

Study, like any activity in Japan worth pursuing, is an opportunity to commit great amounts of effort to a task. The word *benkyoo* (study) in fact connotes the intensity of committed effort required to learn. Study or work is seen as "a positive opportunity to achieve success [rather than] a burden thrust on [one] by circumstances."[1] The success is evident not only in good grades or public recognition of the skills acquired or the products made and sold. Rather, one earns real points through the act of commitment itself. Study, and work of any kind, teaches one about engagement, which has always been the real agenda of learning in Japan.

Japanese modernization and the creation of a modern educational system, while seemingly pursuing goals that appear universal—such as industrial rationalization and productivity and the equal distribution of educational opportunities—took place in a context rather different from what happened in the West. First, educational mobilization—the extension of formal schooling to the entire population—occurred within the structure of social relationships and cultural values about learning that had been in place for hundreds of years. Furthermore, the seeming individual benefits gained from going to school were experienced by groups, particularly the family. Again, personal goals and social linkages were not at odds with each other. Therefore, the job of education in a society fully mobilized to learn is quite different from ours: it is not only to discover and develop personal abilities but to create a set of environments that motivate. The sensible assumption is that highly motivated performance will result in high productivity.

This Japanese understanding of incentive is probably the key to both the institutional and intrinsic equality of Japanese education. When engaged effort is valued over ability, the environment of study or work is more truly egalitarian than it would be if the ceiling on a person's efficacy were set by ability alone. If you commit more hours and more sweat to a task, your identity as a good worker will be enhanced without invidious comparison. Thomas Edison's dictum that genius is "ninety-nine percent perspiration and one percent inspiration" is a precept, like stringent quality control, that seems to work better in Japan though it was coined in the United States. If value is placed on effort, that may be enough to inspire someone to work harder.

The values that helped to shape the modern Japanese educational system also existed in different form in Japanese schools prior to modernization. Yet because there were many types of schools and modes of learning in the Tokugawa period (1600–1868), children's experiences in school varied according to the class and gender of the child—and whether he lived in an urban or rural home.

Parental interest in education was, compared to the same period in the West, very high, but represented another variable in the child's experience of learning. Interest did not always correlate positively with wealth and class, for among some aristocratic samurai families, basic literacy was the only "cognitive" goal and other academic skills were ignored. Instead, tutors trained the children in Confucian ethics and the martial arts. Hence, the use of the abacus and other computational skills were proscribed for samurai youths as unbefitting the upper classes. Children of the emerging middle class in the late Tokugawa period were educated more broadly. They learned the practical skills of computation and literacy, appropriate to a merchant class, and were also instructed in the more refined arts and the ethical precepts of the upper classes they were beginning to emulate.

But for the greater part of almost three hundred years, the most common educational experience for a Japanese child was that of the *terakoya* (the parish school).[2] This was supported locally by the village or town and was first to be found in a temple, where Buddhist priests taught children to read and write. The temple as a source of literacy was so prominent that the word *terako*, "temple child," became synonymous with "student." The content of the education was practical, and its tone, by analogy, consistent with the moral homilies of McGuffey's Readers. Those attending were commoners, most likely farmers' children, and the virtues taught were Japanese agrarian: common sense, cooperation with and respect for others, thrift and the avoidance of waste. While Confucian precepts advocating more stringent observance of filial piety and obedience were part of the curriculum, the morality actually inculcated was homely, and down-to-earth. To get a sense of all this, we can tell a story of an imagined *terako*.

Masa: A *Terako* of Pre-Modern Japan

It is 1850. A boy named Masa, one of five children, lives in a large farmhouse with his parents, his grandparents, and his father's younger sisters in what is now Saitama prefecture, then called Musa-shino, an area near Tokyo. Masa is ten years old, the second son to parents who are thirty-two and thirty. Three of his mother's eight pregnancies ended in early deaths or stillbirths, and she is pregnant again.

Masa's father is the eldest son of his parents, who are in their early fifties. They have not yet "retired" by passing on the management of the farm to their son and the symbolic rice paddle to their daughter-in-law as household manager. Masa's parents defer in all decisions to the older couple, and this affects Masa, since his grandmother completely dominates his mother in matters of the children's care and training. However, the outcome for Masa isn't as harsh as it is for his elder brother and younger siblings, since he is his grandmother's "special child" (*baasan ko*). When his younger sister was born, leaving him no longer the baby of the family, he was "adopted" by his grandmother and thereafter slept on his *futon* beside hers and was fed by her at the table. He also learned to run to her when he was hurt or unhappy. The other children resent this a little, since their ally is only their mother, who cannot finally win in any battle against her mother-in-law.

When the children were infants, they were tightly bound to the mother's back, heads facing her neck; they accompanied Mother every-where. (In other parts of Japan, the practice called *ejikko* leaves infants swaddled and placed in baskets.)

Children do not have a set schedule tied to principles of Western child-rearing (such as meal hours set especially for children or fixed bedtimes), but fit into the adult schedule. Usually Masa does not take leave of adults at the end of the day until he is about to fall asleep; when he was younger, he would simply fall asleep at the hearth and was carried to bed when his grandmother was ready to take him. Masa hears almost every adult conversation and is present at almost every adult event, and, while he is not expected to participate, his presence, along with that of the other children, is taken for granted. Occasionally, but rarely, the adults will hush one another or ask the children to leave if a topic seen as inappropriate to them comes up. The only encounters not observed by children are sexual ones, for their parents take care to restrict their affectionate physical gestures and sexual intercourse to brief moments when the entire household is asleep.

The many adults in the household generally feel free to direct, play with, or even discipline the children, but there is a hierarchical order that determines whose directives hold the most force. The young aunts, for instance, indulge the children and slip them sweets, but they can be overruled by the grandmother, while the one with least to say publicly about their upbringing is the children's own mother. She is at the low end of the ladder of authority, and although it is sometimes acknowledged by the grandmother that she has done well in providing the family with healthy sons, her job is to take care of them for the family, not to assert herself or even have an opinion about the management of the household.

Masa's mother does have her own strategies for coping without overt power. She has learned how to manipulate both her husband and her children to be her allies, although his power to help her is limited by the inappropriateness of his public intercession on her behalf, and her children can only give her affection and "indulge" her by making demands of her, to show that they need her. In any case, most negotiations and interactions are unspoken, and children can sense but not explicitly understand the tensions, alliances, and love of the household.

It is an October day in 1850. The family rises early—the grandmother and mother before dawn, to make the fire, boil the water, and make rice for the midmorning luncheon of rice balls, pickles, and vegetables. Masa is shaken awake by his mother, who tells him that his father wants him to get up fast and help him stack the rice sheaves that are piled in a small field some distance from their house in the village. The weather doesn't look good for completing the harvest today, and Masa hopes that a downpour will come soon enough for him to be able to go to school. In harvest season he and his friends often miss school to help out at home, boys working in the fields, girls taking over domestic tasks at home while their mothers work with the men. The recent spate of fine weather has meant that he hasn't seen his friends for several days. October is generally clear, and he misses his friends greatly at this time of year.

Masa throws water on his face from the basin near the kitchen, pulls on his padded jacket, scuffs his feet into his wooden *geta,* and runs from the house to join his father. The rice sheaves have already been cut and tied by his mother and aunt, and are lying in neat piles along the rows of stubbly cut stalks.

Masa and his father set up bamboo frames, tying the joints with hempen cord, and place the sheaves against the supports. They finish only two frames' worth before the clouds issue rain and they run for home. Masa grabs a rice-ball lunch made by his mother, pulls a rice-straw rain cape over his shoulders and head, and runs to the temple. On the way he meets two of his friends, who have also been released by the weather from their chores. They run together the rest of the way and arrive as the teacher finishes ringing the bell. There are ten children gathered already. The thirteen of them range in age from seven to fourteen. The teacher helps them hang their capes to dry on high hooks, telling them to line up their *geta* in the entrance hall and not leave them in a heap. They chat excitedly, exchanging gossip and complaining about the recent good weather.

Masa's teacher is a retired merchant, whose eldest son took over his shop and who supplements the household's income by teaching. What he earns is payment in kind: his pupils' parents bring him rice, produce, occasionally home-woven cloth or home-made sake, in exchange for his teaching services. He is a little fussy with his charges but understands that their presence, and energy, in school is constrained by parental priorities that may sometimes put schooling second to family needs. He calls the children to order, which in this school's case means settling them on the raised tatami-matted platform near the fire and assigning each a task. The noise level doesn't drop much.

Masa shifts nervously, for he has forgotten the characters for the lines from a Confucian text he is to transcribe, and looks around to see if his friends have remembered. The teacher sees that they are bogged down, and draws the three of them aside to recite instead. He hopes to give them confidence by first choosing something they can do easily before tackling the characters they've forgotten during the harvest.

They recite in unison, and the teacher, listening to them carefully at first, is lulled by their voices and by the steady sound of the rain on the roof. He nods off but shakes himself awake, and with renewed vigor sets them at their task of writing the characters, reviewing the order of strokes with them, and asking them to repeat the task several times.

The day continues in this fashion, lessons assigned according to age and ability, with a lot of individual attention given to the children. After the lunch break there is a brief play period, but because the weather is so bad the children stay inside, near the fire, and the teacher tells them a story.

When school is over, the clouds have dispersed and Masa and

his friends delay returning home. They talk and joke with each other as they walk through the village, splashing in puddles at each other and teasing the girls who are walking in front of them. It has been a very good day, in spite of the temporary embarrassment over the forgotten characters.

Masa was a Japanese child who attended schools in pre-modern, rural Japan. Children in larger towns, or of wealthier parents, spent more time at school than did Masa, and had a richer curriculum. The elements which were remarkably constant for children included the individual attention Masa received, and the personal care offered by his teacher. Before the advent of compulsory schooling, and the mechanization of labor and urbanization, parents saw school as an important part of their children's lives but not as important in their occupational futures—and in any case, even a child of five could perform essential tasks in a productive household. A farm child, especially a boy, reached adult work capacity between the ages of twelve and fifteen, and after that, the skills he was seen to need were further refinement, and common sense, related to tasks he was already doing. Schooling for bureaucratic careers implied a different trajectory and delayed maturation—and most important, took place outside the home and often remote from parental experiences. Apprenticeships in crafts and other trades occurred outside the home, for it was seen as necessary that the child "eat another's rice" (*tanin no meshi o kuu*) in order to receive sufficient discipline to succeed.

THE TRANSITION TO A NATIONAL SYSTEM

The parents of a boy like Masa, and certainly Masa himself, would not have been aware of the event which took place three years after the day we have described, but Masa's children and grandchildren would have experienced great changes in their schooling and lives as a result of the shock of the encounter with the West, beginning in 1853.

The arrival of Admiral Perry's "black ships" in 1853 did not leave Japan quaking and vulnerable. On the contrary, the cohesion which had developed over three centuries of protected isolation allowed Japan to respond with vigor and sufficiently organized confidence to bootstrap itself into the industrialized world.

Changes in the political structure and in social organization after the Meiji Restoration of 1868 were effected with relatively little social upheaval. These were accompanied by reforms aimed at modernizing and centralizing Japan. A national educational system was seen as a crucial step to economic and social modernization, as well as a means for creating the coherence and consensus needed for a nation-state.

Japanese educational planners and elite officials who traveled on special missions to Europe and America in the 1860s and 1870s returned with a variety of educational models and theories. German, Italian, French, and American pedagogical ideas and systems were discussed, and the influences of Pestalozzi, Froebel, and others were incorporated into a system whose organization was French, whose curriculum was American, and whose theories were, for the most part, German.

Japan discovered Western educational theory and practice at a time when many educational systems, such as Prussia's, were strongly tied to nationalism rather than to economic development. Education was seen as the means for developing a citizenry rather than a labor force, though English educators discussed the virtues of inculcating obedience, regular habits, and ideas about the rational use of time through universal education.

Japan's needs, however, were for both political and social cohesion and a rationalized work force for industrialization. The first was to be achieved through the perpetuation of a strong national culture in education, which could protect Japan from Western imperialism. Education was to both preserve and create this culture out of the regionalism and diversity which had previously existed, and would do this through the use of a national curriculum and reference in the schools to national symbols such as the emperor. Despite all the influences brought into the new school system, the first consideration was always that the system be *Japanese*.

The mixture of a Prussian rationale for an imperial education, American progressive education, French organizational acumen, and Confucian ideas about learning was in essence Japanese in the very fact of adaptation, and in the optimistic insistence that there would emerge a modern, educated, yet indisputably Japanese populace. Japanese planners were alert to intended and unintended cultural consequences of national development and saw that if they could control the importation of Western ideas and technology, the goals of cultural integrity and rapid transformation could both be achieved.

In the 1872 Fundamental Code of Education, the last vestiges of a class-based educational system were removed, and schooling for all classes was integrated. The centralization of schooling and the universalization of the experiences of learning depended not only on political and economic decisions at high levels, but also on a very new idea: that all children, of whatever birth and class, possessed the capacity for improvement through a single curriculum and pedagogy. The first goal was universal literacy, as stated in the preamble to the Code: "Learning is the key to success in life. . . . There shall, in the future, be no community with an illiterate family; nor a family with an illiterate person."[3]

While there were problems, and progress toward an acceptable uniform curriculum can be traced through many sharp switchback turns, the success of Japanese educational mobilization was evident. By 1880 there already existed the same number of primary schools as exist today, and by the turn of the century 98 percent of elementary school age children were in school, again the same percentage as is enrolled today.

Education for Everyone

Educational mobilization was carried out in rural areas as well as in the cities. Children in farm families, especially younger sons who would not inherit the farm, were seen to need the occupational advantages afforded by education. One of the effects of the relatively even distribution of education across the population was that there was a less sharp demarcation between rural and urban populations than would have otherwise existed. This helped to facilitate industrialization, since the large numbers of rural youth who came to work in modern factories could adjust easily to the bureaucratic and routinized environment of the plant. Moreover, rural migrants to the cities experienced less shock or alienation, and there was less social distinction between literate urbanites and illiterate country bumpkins than that which has usually been found in developing societies.

Government scholarships were provided for young people to attend normal schools for training as teachers, with the aim of encouraging poor and rural youth especially. While Meiji-period education is often seen as emphasizing the creation of a political and technologically sophisticated elite, the sheer numbers of children and young persons sponsored or subsidized meant that education had emerged as a mass phenomenon. In any case there was relatively open access to an education which might, for a poor but ambitious youth, provide the basis for a prominent career—and for those who couldn't enter universities, a middle or high school education and inventive flair could lead to the top in private industry and commerce.

"Boys, be ambitious!" was the exhortation offered by a visiting American teacher, William Clark, who visited Sapporo in the late nineteenth century, and who inspired a generation with his homespun American call for upward social mobility. *Risshin shusse,* "Raise yourself and make your way in the world" was indeed such a Japanized goal, buttressed by the great popularity of the messages of such books as Samuel Smiles's *Self Help,* a best-seller in the Meiji period.

Enterprise and drive were seen at all levels. The new Western learning had attracted many lower samurai, especially younger sons, frustrated with their circumscribed chances in life during the late Tokugawa period. More generally, the groundwork had been laid for an explosion of talent across the population. Yukichi Fukuzawa, who was later to become the founder of Keio University, a famous private university in Tokyo, wrote of his early youth as a renegade scholar and his escape from the narrow constraints of his father's feudal heritage. His motivation to study seems to have arisen from his frustration with his life in his mother's natal home on Kyushu: "I would have been glad to study a foreign language or the military art or anything else if it only gave me a chance to go away."[4]

Fukuzawa worked hard and passionately at anything Dutch—since that was the medium through which Western learning was trickling into Japan. He learned gunnery and medicine, since those were two subjects on which Dutch materials were available. He transcribed whole books, since there were few copies. And he once worked for twenty days straight to make an illicit copy of a manual on defensive fortifications, so eager was he to work in Western languages. Raised on the Chinese classics that encouraged the development of goodness through study and taught the ascetic virtues of his samurai progenitors that gave him the will to commit great effort, Fukuzawa is a clear example of the Japanese capacity to adapt key traditional values to new historical settings.

As a younger son in a fatherless household, Fukuzawa had no great prospects, nor could education per se help him to rise in a society in which there was no mobility. His father had intended him for the priesthood, in which there was some chance for self-betterment, but as he did not live to enact and enforce his plan, the son was left to find his own route.

Fukuzawa was raised by models and dicta. Frequently, ancient or contemporary men were cited as exemplars of virtue. A retainer of the shogun, Egawa Tarozaemon, was said to have such self-control that he wore only summer clothing all winter long. Fukuzawa heard the story when he was fourteen, and decided to emulate him by sleeping all winter in a single thin blanket, even while his mother was understandably very anxious for him.

Fukuzawa, however, had no intention of becoming a traditional samurai, and laughed when his elder brother gave a strict rendering of the proper life: "I will be dutiful to my parents, faithful to my brethren, and loyal to my master until death."[5] His own interpretation of the proper life did involve personal tests of endurance, but his asceticism was not based in samurai pride alone, but in a drive to accomplish personal goals. His brother was soon to be an anachronism, but Fukuzawa turned the scriptural virtues of the samurai into more portable "modern" qualities which could transcend the social barriers erected by the old values.

Education Before World War II

From the end of the Meiji period (1912) to World War II, Japanese education experienced a widely diverse set of influences. John Dewey was particularly in vogue in the 1920s. His influence was strong in part because while his proposals could clearly be seen as modern and Western, they were in their underlying philosophy close to indigenous Japanese ideas of the unity of cognitive, physical, and affective development. The roots for the idea of educating the "whole child," which returned with American occupation reforms after the war, were deeply Japanese, and because of their Western cachet could flourish as a modern "import." Dewey's first impact, however, was a philosophic one, with some influence on experimental education.

Education in the prewar era of the 1930s was closely tied to the national mobilization for war. Because of the need to harness nationalistic sentiment and because of the fear that education and society at large had been too greatly influenced by Western culture, a "re-Japanization" of the educational system was begun. This meant a strong ideological component incorporated across the curriculum, the elimination of most foreign language instruction, except in a few "protected" schools, and the introduction of newly restructured morals courses.

In the latter part of the war, many schools in large cities were closed altogether, because most children had been relocated to the countryside to protect them from bombings and because most teachers were part of the war effort. Children from middle schools and high schools were often recruited by classes into factories, including munitions plants. A class, together with its teacher, would work as a unit in a plant, and the experience is often remembered with nostalgic pleasure, for these children were well treated and were working with their friends in a novel and highly motivated endeavor. However, the situation for non-middle-class children working in mines and factories and not recruited through the schools is reported to have been one of great exploitation and hardship.[6] We know that in the West the wartime shortage of men drew women into the labor force. In Japan children, rather than their mothers, were recruited to fill the gap. This was consistent with Japanese values.

By the end of the war, there was virtually no coherent schooling. Moreover, there had been a nearly ten-year hiatus in the teaching of several elements of the curriculum, and those of high school age at the end of the war are now considered a generation with serious gaps in its formal education. It is these people who, in large numbers, worked for the American Occupation, and were seen by older Japanese as culturally deprived and rootless: they became, in spite of knowing little really about the West, a marginal "Westernized" group, and as such devalued by mainstream Japanese. For them, the Occupation and its Western opportunities were the only paths available. The more successful of the marginal group became the "self-made men" who helped to create the postwar economic boom of the 1960s.

When the bottom fell out after Japan lost World War II, schools became the only secure source of a future for children, and, as in the Meiji period, the need for schools as institutions to develop children for the nation's rebuilding became central in Japanese planning. Parents were now ready to invest themselves emotionally in their children, and this replaced the commitment to a Japanese victory in war.

THE AMERICANIZATION OF THE JAPANESE SCHOOL

For those still of school age at the end of the war, the educational system created by the Occupation presented a very different structure

and environment from that which they had known. Compulsory schooling was extended to nine years (elementary and junior high schools);
the 6–3–3–4 division of schooling was adopted; and coeducation was
made universal in public schools. The content of the curriculum was
thoroughly scrutinized for militaristic and nationalistic elements and
the morals course was scrapped. For a while, even Japanese history
and geography courses were suspended.

As in the educational changes of the nineteenth century, reform
of the content of the postwar curriculum posed little problem; it was
the restructuring of educational *institutions* which strained society's
adaptive powers. While abstract concepts such as "democratic values"
were well received after the war, the concrete decentralization of
school bureaucracies, among other changes, met resistance. However,
with few substantive changes, at least initially, the American model
was adopted, and local school boards, the P-TA, and the Teachers'
Union became fixtures in the environment of the school. In fact, the
latter two organizations have become more powerful and active in
their transplanted forms than in the American originals: the P-TA as
a kind of ritualized therapy "club" for anxious mothers, as well as
a training ground for women learning to take roles in public activities;
and the Teachers' Union as the largest union in Japan, characterized
by its strong leftist opposition to the ministry of education and to
the mainstream establishment at large.

Before the war, the ritualized reading of the Imperial Rescript
on Education had been an important part of the school day. Occupation
officials saw it as nationalistic, probably more because of the reverence
with which it was treated than because of its content. However, even
though it emphasized devotion to the person of the emperor as a
sort of national "father," it did not immediately disappear. Japanese
educators defended its retention by saying that the "vertical" loyalty
and "horizontal" harmony it extolled were important cultural sources
of strength needed in Japan's peaceful reconstruction and that the
militarists had distorted its value by using it as an object of imperial
devotion. Several alternatives were suggested. But by the end of 1946,
the Rescript, and its potential revisions, were all eliminated. The
Japanese postwar school had fewer ritual invocations than did the
American school, where the daily Pledge of Allegiance and the Lord's
Prayer could still be heard.

Japanese educators, in an attempt to see the postwar democratiza-
tion of education as an extension of indigenous values and practices,
stressed the "egalitarian" relationship of teacher and student. This

they saw as consonant with Japanese tradition, which values the warmth and affection in the bond. Gunzo Kojima, a postwar educational theorist, devised the phrase *kyoiku-ai* (love in education) and described this love as follows:

> It is love in educational activities which generates the driving force of the teacher's action toward the learner in terms of personality and which gives vitality to guidance. [The first kind of love is] . . . the natural human love which is common in other aspects of human life and which the teacher has always in his heart as he . . . watches the sound growth of the immature and inexperienced pupil . . . the second is a conscious love with which the teacher finds within the pupil the potentials for an ideal person, and endeavors for this fulfillment with sincere hope.[7]

In the traditional relationship it is said that the love between teacher and student is accompanied by and exhibited in discipline and morality. The combination makes the relationship one of respect but not of distance. In other words, traditional "vertical" relationships could be seen as primarily benevolent rather than authoritarian or exploitative, and "democracy" could be seen as consonant with the spirit, if not the structure, of relationships of the past. Here one of the mechanisms of Japanese adaptation can be seen. Without rewriting history, an emphasis could be placed on elements of the preexisting values and social structure which could support or complement an innovation, and aspects of the innovation which could most easily be coordinated with the existing environment would be emphasized.

Choosing education as the backbone of postwar social reform, the Occupation devoted energy to what the Japanese themselves consider the focal institution for individual and social development. Well before school was a source of credentials for a child's occupational future or life chances in general, the Japanese had strongly felt that creating literacy and wider schooling was the responsibility of society toward its children. While the function of the educational system to select the most able was evident in the later stages of industrialization, that function has, if anything, become even important in a society now virtually 100 percent literate, in which 94 percent of children go beyond compulsory education to finish high school and 34 percent finish college.

In summary, since the Meiji Restoration, the motivation for a unified national educational system can be traced to three factors:

1. A concern for children and their social and cognitive development
2. A policy level interest in modernization which regarded education as an indicator of Japan's progress in the international world

3. A recognition that industry, commerce, and the running of efficient and productive bureaucracies depend on loyalty and motivation for high performance, outcomes which the Japanese had long considered important products of education

In other words, the Meiji-period push for a centralized educational system and the postwar readiness to stress education as key to social reconstruction have their roots in the same consensus that schooling and learning provide the individual with necessary skills and the society with a trained and motivated citizenry.

4

JAPANESE SCHOOLS TODAY

Japanese children today go to schools which very much resemble those of the West, at least superficially, but the similarities are only a single brick deep. The alchemy making the borrowed model into an indigenous cultural phenomenon has by now completely transformed the Occupation-period ''American'' education into schooling fully congruent with Japanese goals and mores. A look at practices, schedules, and the environment of the classroom will show us some of the dimensions of difference.

A Japanese child *must* be in school between the ages of six and fifteen, or the elementary and junior high school years. This much is guaranteed for all children. In fact, however, children typically enter formal schooling at three or four, in private nursery schools, and 94 percent of them finish high school.

The school year begins on April 1 and ends at the end of March the following year. There are three terms: April through July, September through December, and January through March. There are about 240 school days per year. Classes are held for half a day on Saturdays, although there have been several efforts to eliminate them. Efforts have so far failed because of objections on the part of parents to the implied abdication of the schools.

The school calendar has many special days, organized around projects such as science fairs and class trips. Field trips are a regular part of the life of a schoolchild, and major class trips (*shugaku-ryoko*), held often during the summer vacation, are not to be missed. All grades go on day trips, but by the fifth and sixth grades children are taken on excursions with at least one overnight stay. The children stay in Japanese-style inns, where the boys share one large room and the girls another. They sleep on *futon*s spread on the tatami-matted floor, and the evenings are like wild slumber parties. The next day usually finds the children bleary-eyed. This is the first time most children have traveled without a parent and often the first time they have left their own part of Japan. The class may ride the bullet train to Kyoto or Hiroshima, or may go by bus to scenic rural areas. Children are carefully prepared for weeks beforehand in both the sights to be seen and the expectations for their behavior.

The occasions are very special ones, remembered at reunions for decades. Children who for some reason, such as serious illness or a death in the family, cannot go always remember the tragedy of being left out of the fun.

Schools are spare, by American standards physically unattractive, but still pleasant places. Typically they are constructed in concrete in L- or U-shaped formations, partially enclosing a schoolyard, where morning assembly, recess games, and sports classes and demonstrations are held. There may also be a school garden, where the children themselves grow vegetables and flowers, a bicycle-parking area, and, tucked in a patch of shrubbery or outside the main entrance, a statue of Ninomiya Sontoku.

Inside the two- or three-story building, there are long corridors with classrooms along one side, windows along the other. The walls often need plastering and paint. There are many displays of the children's work, often exhibits appropriate to the season, prepared by the children. The classroom furnishings are not fancy either, and yet the rooms are lively and light, for the walls are covered with children's artwork, and there are usually many windows along which there may also be plants and projects created by the children.

The younger the children, the less fixed are the furnishings, for teachers like to move the desks of elementary school children into various patterns, depending on the task at hand and the social configuration thought most appropriate to it. In high schools, there are typically rows of two desks side by side, with aisles between each pair. In elementary school, girls and boys sit together, but by junior high the sexes tend to cluster.

The atmosphere of the classroom is very lively, even noisy. A class will have an average of forty-two children to one teacher. The teacher's main concern is that the children be engaged in their work, and not that they be disciplined or docile. Thus, an American teacher might be distressed at the decibel level tolerated.

The large student–teacher ratio means that expectations for pupil behavior and instructor intervention are different from those we would expect. As Joseph Tobin suggests,[1] the Japanese teacher delegates more authority to children than we find in American schools; intervenes less quickly in arguments; has lower expectations for the control of noise generated by the class; gives fewer verbal cues; organizes more structured large-group activities, such as morning exercise; and, finally, makes more use of peer-group approval and control and less of the teacher's direct influence. In general, children are less often treated on a one-to-one basis, and more often as a group.

Japanese students are almost always promoted with their age group, rarely advanced or held back by ability. A prolonged illness might keep a child from moving on, but his absence from the group and from its shared experiences would be at issue as much as having fallen behind in coursework.

During the time the Japanese student is required to be in school, the curriculum emphasizes creating a uniform base for further development of skills and abilities. There is little room for "electives." Where the latter exist, the most often chosen is English, which has in some schools become all but compulsory by junior high school. Morals classes have returned as "moral education" or in Christian and Buddhist private schools as "religious instruction."

The following tables show the hours spent during a single year in various elementary and lower secondary subject areas. A class "hour" is forty-five minutes in elementary school and fifty in junior high. Some classes, such as science laboratory classes, are double sessions, and have a ten-minute break between them.

For intensity, Japanese language classes top the list: the large numbers of characters to be learned require a great deal of memorization and drill not exhibited in the rest of the curriculum. By the end of elementary school, approximately one thousand characters must be learned—both to read and write—and by the end of junior high school, nineteen hundred characters, or the minimum for literacy as determined by the ministry of education. Mathematics and physical education are also areas of concentration. In mathematics, creative problem-solving is emphasized among elementary and lower secondary pupils as well as a solid grounding in various mathematical processes.

TABLE 1
Standard Number of Yearly School Hours in Elementary School

Subject	1	2	3	Grade 4	5	6
Japanese	272	280	280	280	210	210
Social studies	68	70	105	105	105	105
Arithmetic	136	175	175	175	175	175
Science	68	70	105	105	105	105
Music	68	70	70	70	70	70
Arts	68	70	70	70	70	70
Homemaking[1]	—	—	—	—	70	70
Phys. ed.	102	105	105	105	105	105
Moral ed.	34	35	35	35	35	35
Other[2]	34	35	35	70	70	70
Totals	850	910	980	1,015	1,015	1,015

Table derived from *Basic Facts and Figures About the Educational System in Japan* (Tokyo: National Institute for Educational Research, 1982), 16–17.
[1] For both boys and girls.
[2] Such as assemblies, club activities, guidance.

TABLE 2
Standard Number of Yearly School Hours in Junior High School

Subject	1	Grade 2	3
Japanese	175	140	140
Social studies	140	140	105
Math	105	140	140
Science	105	105	140
Music	70	70	35
Arts	70	70	35
Phys. ed.	105	105	105
Ind. arts and homemaking[1]	70	70	105
Moral ed.	35	35	35
Other[2]	70	70	70
Electives	105	105	140
Totals	1,050	1,050	1,050

Table derived from *Basic Facts and Figures About the Educational System in Japan* (Tokyo: National Institute for Educational Research, 1982), 16–17.
[1] For both boys and girls
[2] Such as assemblies, club activities, and guidance.

Working with computers does not play much of a role in the Japanese school. Only 0.58 percent of Japanese elementary schools use computers, compared with 22 percent of American schools; even more striking, the rate is only 3.09 percent in Japanese junior high schools and 52 percent in American junior high schools. At high school levels, the rate is 56.4 percent in Japan and 74 percent in the United States.

The calculator is used in Japan but hasn't replaced mental calculations, or, for some, the abacus. In short, there seems to be no national program to develop skills in high technology among children. One third-grade math teacher, when asked why her charges didn't use the school's computers, responded by saying "Class time is too precious to use machines." Americans spend much more time and money on technology in the schools, and less, overall, on enhancing the environment and the skill of the teacher.

In contrast to American schools, serious homework is assigned to the Japanese first grader, who gets more and more of it as he moves on. By the time a child is in high school, he or she spends several hours a day on homework. In sum, 65 percent of Japanese students spend more than five hours per week on homework; the figure is 24 percent for American seniors.[2]

RESPONSIBILITY FOR THE CHILD: HOME AND SCHOOL

Compared to the United States, the Japanese responsibility for engendering the healthy development of the young person is more diffusely shared by family, school, and workplace.[3] For example, schoolteachers, principals, and parents, as well as the young person himself, are called to account by the police when a high school student is picked up for driving without a license. And besides the teacher's efforts, parents are expected to provide daily assistance with homework. In a recent poll, data indicates that mothers are consulted more frequently than any other adult, including teachers, on academic work. Meanwhile, high schools and colleges take an active role in finding jobs for their graduates. After entering a company, a young person can expect his or her superiors to help in the individual and parental search for a suitable wife or husband. Some companies even sponsor the wedding ceremonies. Clearly, responsibility for important aspects of personal development is not only allocated differently in Japan, but is also simultaneously assumed by several different parties.

Accordingly, Japanese schools and Japanese parents are both fully engaged in children's social and moral conduct as well as their academic progress, and schools provide active assistance integrating their graduates into the next phase of life. The persistence of this engagement may stem from the tradition of shared responsibility found in apprenticeship systems and small-scale agrarian communities. But while the influence of such traditions is undoubtedly present, the contemporary form of a shared role for child rearing is not much different from the general pattern found in other areas of life.

The pattern means that if an accident occurs in school (or on the job), blame can be less directly ascribed. But because an untoward event may be identified with a large group or network of people or even an institution, the improper behavior of one person brings negative consequences to bear on a large number of people. So while a sense of security is achieved through shared responsibility, the effects of a sin of commission or omission on one's social network are a serious deterrent to individual irresponsibility.

American schools also feel that they are accountable for the academic progress and the physical safety of their students. And parents feel that both may be enforced as if they constituted a contract: if a school is negligent, the parents may expect redress. An exaggerated example of the assumption may be seen in recent lawsuits brought by parents against schools for failing to educate their children.

Japanese and American preparations for a school field trip show further differences in the nature and determination of responsibility. In America a teacher will talk about the academic lessons to be derived from the trip and ask students to have parents sign forms releasing the school from legal responsibility in case of a mishap. But social etiquette and proper cooperative behavior rarely merit more than a passing comment because they are regarded as the responsibility of the parents.

Japanese schools, however, are concerned not only with academic progress and physical safety but with social behavior. Permission slips are not used, because physical safety is believed to be the proper responsibility of everyone involved: the child, classmates, the teacher, the person in charge of the place of the visit, the principal, and to some degree the parents as well. A school that might try using permission slips would be considered socially and probably morally deficient.

This means the entire class must carefully discuss safety precautions and the behavior expected of all of them. The responsibility of the students to the school's image, to other people in public places, to their classmates, and to their parents is explicitly talked through. And those in direct authority—principal, teachers, and class monitors—lay out procedures and precautions to be observed. In sum, with overlapping responsibilities and careful preparation, the likelihood of a mishap is reduced and the number of people who will share in the consequences of a mishap greatly increased.

Thus, if a Japanese child were to fall from a train platform while on a field trip, self-recriminations and apologies would be expected from everyone involved. The child, the class monitors, the teacher, the principal, would all apologize to each other and to the parents; the parents would then apologize to the school for the unruliness of their child; and the railway stationmaster would apologize for whatever deficiencies might have existed. The social effects of the mishap would not end there: A feeling of *meiwaku o kaketa* (having caused trouble for someone) would suffuse all of the relationships for some time, and most likely a continuing exchange of gifts and favors would occur to redress the wrongs.

The heightened sense of collective responsibility means that people try very hard through preventive measures and conservative behavior to reduce the possibility of something going wrong. If something does, prompt and even (to a Westerner) exaggerated assumption of responsibility is regarded as exemplary behavior which enhances one's social stature and which can redress some of the damage caused to one's image. Another reality here is that Japanese tend to feel that blame is more difficult to assign to someone who is visibly suffering guilt and who has already inflicted upon himself some type of punishment. Such a demonstration by one who is not actually responsible is sometimes calculated to arouse feelings of guilt in the one more directly at fault. This behavioral mode is used by parents to discourage irresponsible behavior in their children, and by others in positions of authority to encourage the loyal cooperation of their employees or subordinates.

To Western observers, the diffuse sharing of blame (and credit) appears to minimize individual accountability and therefore to encourage bad behavior. In fact, the diffusion of responsibility in the West would diminish the incentive to keep one's socks up. But in Japan the *combination* of spreading involvement and invoking indebtedness works. Failure thus can affect a network of people and increase a sense of indebtedness to one's kin, colleagues, and superiors. And because this might happen, careful, responsible behavior is greatly encouraged. In general, the interlocking, overlapping, mutually reinforcing responsibilities shared by the family, school, and company for the development of the individual is an important factor behind the success of Japanese education.

THE PRODUCT

It has now become standard to talk about education in economic terms. To quantify the benefits and costs of Japanese schools, we are given test scores and suicide rates. But this is obviously not enough, and to understand where the data come from, we need to look at context more carefully.

The international media are thoroughly familiar with the high test scores of Japanese children. The scores generally exceed those of children in the West. Moreover, the Japanese educational system also scores high in international comparisons in terms of the numbers of children engaged in formal learning, the time they spend at it, and the place education has in someone's life chances. The children also, in greater numbers than elsewhere, report that they *like* school.

The curriculum—the courses taken and the material covered—is so rich that a high school diploma in Japan can be said to be the equivalent of a college degree in the United States. In math and sciences, particularly, Japanese children receive a broad and comprehensive education. It has recently been shown that the lowest math and science test scores in fifth grade classes in Japan are higher than the highest test scores in comparable American schools.[4]

Significant also is the fact that there is less variation in performance across the population than in most other societies.[5] Indeed it is a source of some wonder in Japan that children elsewhere do not perform as well and that standards and incentives in other advanced nations are so low. In other words, "high achievement" has become a standard expectation in Japan.

The effects of this situation are evident well after the end of formal schooling, for widespread literacy is accompanied by widespread engagement in all forms of knowledge-enhancing activities across all sectors of the population. There is a high level of cultural engagement as well: blue-collar workers submit original classical verse to newspaper columns. Moreover, the national media use highly sophisticated technical vocabularies, and it is assumed that everyone can read music.

So what are the costs and benefits of the achievement? To evaluate them, both Japanese and Western perspectives must be taken into account. Observers from both East and West tend to come down hard on the toll exacted by the exams for entrance to high school and college. "Examination hell," the weeks or months of grueling effort preparing for an examination, does in fact put a significant number of young people under a significant amount of pressure. Whether or not this produces psychologically damaging stress varies from one young person to another. But some effects do seem to influence the lives of most young people.

First, as a youngster approaches the end of junior high school he has less and less free time; even those who are not taking after-school classes, being tutored, or just spending the hours in independent study have fewer peers with whom to spend that time. Nearly everyone can be found either in a structured activity or devoted to solitary pastimes such as watching TV or playing video games. Second, the young person approaching exams or decisions affecting his future is no longer a member of a relatively undifferentiated and supportive group. He is now to be measured and selected as an individual, and, however well the moment of selection is buffered by the continuing nurturant relationships with family and teachers, the experience is strikingly different from what the young person has earlier known.

However, the excesses of examination hell and the pathological outcomes for some do not threaten all. The Western view is that Japanese youth are uniformly engaged in a do-or-die struggle—an image heightened by attention given to the annual juvenile suicide rate, the incidence of school phobia and psychosomatic illnesses, and the prevalence of the "education mama." The Japanese media also emphasize violence in the classroom and at home, the existence of motorcycle gangs, and the (highly organized) rock dancing in a Tokyo street on Sunday afternoons. These are given as evidence of an educational system turned pressure cooker, with the struggle to get ahead having produced an excessively competitive and demoralized generation.

At the same time, Japanese observers of Japanese society are preoccupied with strains in the social fabric which to Americans seem relatively unthreatening. Statistically, neither juvenile suicides nor violence and crime appear to Americans to warrant the critical attention they have received in Japan. When dyeing one's hair or lengthening a skirt are counted as acts of school violence, a standard other than American is being applied. For perspective, one can say that the number of student assaults on teachers in New York City alone in the first semester of the 1974–1975 school year was three times the number of assaults in the entire 1976 school year in all of Japan.[6] It is, however, exactly the critical attention, often heightened by newspaper sensationalism, that feeds the sensitivity shown by Japanese to potential problems—a sensitivity that has created the success of the educational system. Remember that the Japanese feel they are living very precariously on a group of narrow islands and must hence maximize human resources and potential. Because by their lights this is best done through education, there is great concern over how children fare and a disposition to anticipate and attend to any problems that might conceivably arise.

Maximizing Personal Success

The clear net plus for society of the educational system must be weighed against the effect of the educational experience on an individual person's life. In general, Japanese education tries to maximize a child's ability and performance through the collaboration of people, priorities, and processes at many levels. The questions of how the schools stream and screen, how they maintain social cohesion while encouraging each child to work hard to achieve personal success, are best answered by looking at the consonance of goals and means in the home, school, and policymaking institutions.

Japanese and outside observers agree that Japan's rapid development in the Meiji period and the postwar economic miracle are closely related to the emphasis on education. The general level of skill in society was raised, and the especially talented were given a way to rise to positions of influence. During two times of crisis in Japanese history, there was a close correlation between what was good for personal development and what was good for the nation.

Today the finely honed system of selection for the most coveted jobs is still regarded as a sine qua non to the continued stability of Japan. Not only high in status, the positions are highly demanding and require high levels of skill and effort. Because academic success in school is for the Japanese a good indicator of success in such jobs, the school system does the selecting. Accordingly, parents strongly feel that schools must provide their children with everything possible to help them climb the occupational ladder. In Japan few opportunities exist to change paths or retool; the American idea that you can re-create yourself at any time in life, that life is full of second chances, that the self-made person can get ahead, is in no way a Japanese reality. The intensity of examination hell results from both the need to restrict competition to one point in life and from a strong consensus on what the life course is and what its goals should be.

Nevertheless, selecting talent and preserving harmony cannot be done in the same classroom. The need to maintain both has produced a split in the educational system, but one which seems composed of complementary rather than conflicting elements. The regular classroom is a place where the individual does not stick out, where active competition is not encouraged but individual needs are met and goals are set. The cohesion of the age group is paramount. Teachers spend time working with the slower learners, rather than streaming the class to suit different abilities. Moreover, teachers and the school system mostly refuse to become party to examination hysteria, partly because of pressure from the Teachers' Union. This is a very large and powerful labor union that consistently resists any move away from the egalitarian mode of instruction. The union feels that turning teachers into drill instructors would be dehumanizing, and cramming for the examination a poor substitute for learning.

The *Juku*

Where, then, is the principle of competitive selection served? It is served in the *juku,* or private after-school class. For the Japanese child, extracurricular lessons of many sorts are a very common component of the educational experience.[7] Of these, there are two major types: *okeikogoto* (enrichment lessons) and *juku* (supplementary help in academic subjects). *Okeikogoto* frequently begin during the preschool years and may continue throughout one's life. Most classes vary according to fads and the age of the students involved, yet almost all Japanese find themselves in such classes at some time in their lives. Preschool children take lessons like swimming, piano, or English; middle-aged women learn knitting, tennis, or cooking; and retired men study Japanese singing, golf, or tea ceremony. Ways to enrich leisure, they are more common during periods of life when other responsibilities such as formal study, small children, or career are less pressing.

The other type of extracurricular endeavor, *juku,* is taken exclusively during the elementary and secondary school years. Most Japanese children attend some type of *juku* in some major academic subject; in urban areas, 86 percent of ninth grade children report having attended a *juku* at some time. The term loosely covers all extracurricular lessons devoted to academic subjects; however, the range of educational settings and goals is very broad.

Juku range from small classes of two or three students meeting in the home of a teacher to large schools with dozens of classes, hundreds of students and branches all over the country. The content of the courses ranges from remedial to highly accelerated. Some are synchronized with school courses, some are given over to material one or two months ahead of the school curriculum, and some concentrate on techniques and information most likely to earn a high score on entrance exams. Hence the purpose of a course may vary from simply raising a child's math grade to preparing for a specific entrance exam to a targeted prestigious national university.

In urban areas, there are large *juku* with a businesslike and competitive atmosphere mostly attended by students preparing for the university entrance exams. However, many urban *juku,* especially those for elementary and junior high school students, are more informal, given over to the immediate improvement of school performance. The same is true for most *juku* in smaller metropolitan and rural areas, which are much smaller, with seven to fifteen students per class. The larger, examination-oriented *juku* are sometimes also known as *gakushu juku, yobiko,* or *zemina* (from the English ''seminar''). These last two sometimes refer not only to after-school classes but to full-time cram schools attended by *ronin,* those who have graduated from high school but are doing extra work to take or retake college exams.

Besides being a multimillion-dollar industry, *juku* and *okeikogoto* form an unaccredited and unregulated yet indispensable adjunct to the formal educational system. Their proliferation is a natural response to the pressures created by discrepancies between the goals of individual families, the egalitarian ideology, and the structuring of the formal school system. The situation is further complicated by differences between the nature of the curriculum approved by the ministry of

education for use in elementary and secondary schools and the preparation necessary to enter good universities. The tension stems ultimately
from the basic ambivalence in Japanese cultural attitudes between
egalitarianism and hierarchical distinctions.

Individual Ability and the Harmony of the Group

The place of ranked distinctions and competition within an ideology
based on harmony is also reflected in the highly politicized debate
between the ministry of education and the Teachers' Union. The latter
has had a great effect on both classroom practice and ministry-estab-
lished curriculum. As mentioned previously, the union resists any
attempt to turn the ordinary egalitarian school into an agent of meritocratic selection. Schools remain characterized by harmony and not by
competition—in part because of the union's power and in part because
of the *juku,* which provide the battleground, at a safe distance from
traditional institutions, on which the competition necessary to sustain
a modern occupational system can occur.

Differences in ability may produce serious discomfort where social
cohesion must have precedence. Accordingly, social situations are
carefully structured to minimize obvious differences between students
of the same age, or superior ability shown by younger people in
comparison to those a few years older. In their strenuous effort to
minimize invidious distinctions between individual students, modern
schools are similar to the *terakoya* of the Tokugawa period. Unlike
education in the Tokugawa period, however, contemporary education
has become the officially accepted and widely accessible means for
families to try to improve their social status.

BUT ARE THEY CREATIVE?

If a Western educator observed either the ordinary schools or
the *juku,* he would conclude that Japanese education could never
allow the flowering of creativity. That conclusion is at least partly
the result of ethnocentric assumptions about the source and meaning
of creativity. And because Western beliefs about the nature and importance of creativity influence the ways in which we evaluate Japanese
education, we should think for a moment about what we mean by
creativity and why we regard it so highly.[8]

Western folk and academic psychology both contend that creativity is a desirable individual trait. Popular psychology asserts that children possess the potential for considerable creativity, which may diminish as they grow older. Education that is too rigid and the imposition of adult standards too early are frequently cited as the culprits in a child's loss of a presumed spontaneously unacademic way of looking at the world. At the same time, psychologists frequently describe creativity as a statistically rare response or an extraordinary accomplishment, which by definition means that the average child or average adult is not creative.

Moreover, even as Western educators plan curricula for creativity, we believe that creative invention cannot be fostered institutionally. This idea comes from both nineteenth-century romanticism and twentieth-century expressionism. In the latter, the child is to be completely unrestrained and left to his or her own nature. He is to be driven by a naive force of self-expression, what some have called the "immaculate perception."

Some children are taught that spontaneity is more important than skill. I once observed an American gym class where children were given basketballs and told to "get to know" the ball, to understand its nature—a prospect which made some children intensely uncomfortable, since they really wanted to learn how to dribble and shoot. A recent cartoon in *The New Yorker* captures "free spirit" education. A small child, disgruntled, says to a teacher, "Do we have to do what we want to do again today?" Meanwhile, from the romantics we are given to understand that the best creative effort comes to the artist through the inspiration of the *divinus furor,* the "divine fury" that visits the worthy creator from heaven.

Americans, in short, confuse self-expression with creativity, placing the greatest value on spontaneity rather than on taking pains. A contradiction may lurk here. We think, on the one hand, that hard work sometimes leads to creative success—hard work that goes on apart from formal schooling; on the other hand, we persist in the belief that schools can and should develop children's creativity.

Why do Americans especially believe creativity is so important? Part of the answer lies in American preoccupation with individual differences and the accompanying belief that absolutely unique accomplishments are better than those which somehow resemble the efforts of others. We also feel that society moves forward on breakthroughs, on the innovations and discoveries of people like Henry Ford and Albert Einstein.

Why, then, does Japanese creativity (or lack of it) interest Americans so much? Part of the interest may stem from old-fashioned American chauvinism and the need to find Japanese success fundamentally flawed. We cast about for some intangible yet crucial capacity that we have but that is absent in Japanese mentality, society, and education, which in turn will somehow permit us to retain, or regain, the upper hand.

So Americans insist that Japanese can only imitate because we feel that Japanese social structure and values do not provide fertile ground in which creativity can arise. Japanese culture puts much less emphasis on individual than on group accomplishments, and encourages perceptions of similarities rather than differences among individuals' social and cognitive achievements. Accordingly, the argument goes, classroom teachers do not expect a child to develop a novel approach or contribution and instead foster the development of memorization. Young people defer to their teachers well after their schooling has ended. Moreover, until recent American criticism made the Japanese somewhat self-conscious, there was little explicit rhetoric about the importance of creativity in education.

Traditional forms of learning—in crafts and arts—emphasize what we might call old-style creativity in Japan. Apprentices and novices may spend years sweeping the floors, washing vegetables, preparing the master's brushes, clapping out rhythms, before they shape clay, prepare a meal, draw, or try to dance themselves. Even as their performances become fully fluent, the goal remains precise imitation of the master. The fully mature Noh actor may begin to innovate, but this would be scarcely noticeable except to himself, the master, and the true aficionado—a slight turn of the head, a refinement of a movement of the hand. Such innovations, like a tiny modification of the glaze on a pot or the use of a new flower in a stylized arrangement, are in fact creative acts, which, among the right audience, produce the ''Ah!'' of shocked recognition that is experienced anywhere in the world in the presence of something truly creative.

The school, however, is a place where a new kind of creativity can be fostered. Japanese schools are, like most of ours, routinized. But because positive engagement and enthusiasm are emphasized, even what an American would call creativity is elicited in certain classes. The outcomes of *Japanese* routinization are, surprisingly, a high degree of analytic and creative problem-solving, as well as expressions of divergent points of view.

In arts education particularly, America cannot accuse Japanese schools of neglecting to foster creativity. In Japanese schools art is not a frill, it is basic. As Diane Ravitch says, for the Japanese the "development of an aesthetic sense" is as important as "learning about nature."[9] Hence all Japanese children learn to play two instruments and read music as part of the required elementary school curriculum. Moreover, every child participates in dramatic productions and receives instruction in drawing and painting. The belief is that before a child can be truly creative, or even express himself, he must be taught possibilities and limits of the medium; in short, one learns how to use the existing forms first. Americans who have observed Japanese children in arts classes also point to the group nature of instruction, and incorrectly assume that only as soloists, composers, and individual artists can they be truly creative—a perception highly colored by our own view of what creativity means.

Criticism leveled at Japanese education also comes down on what is seen as a suppression of genius. There is indeed little provision for tracking the superbright to their best advantage, but their best advantage may be defined very differently in Japan and America. A very bright child, appropriately socialized, will soon enough receive appropriate rewards in Japan, but he is not expected to burst through the limits established by others. He is unlike his American counterpart, who is expected to break records very early in life.

In sum, it will not get us very far to claim that the Japanese have successfully trained children to take exams at the expense of a broader education. And it is not at all appropriate to say that they cannot develop children's individuality and encourage the geniuses who make scientific breakthroughs. The first is untrue, and as for the second, the Japanese, formidable organizers that they are, are now mobilizing themselves to produce scientists and technologists who will show themselves to be creative by anyone's measure. In my judgment, the scales now appear to be tipped in favor of Japan.

5

A PARADISE FOR TEACHERS?

The American teacher may well envy his Japanese counterpart. He is well respected, secure in his job, and well paid. The school administrator here also might envy the Japanese principal, whose staff meet his goals and expectations and whose direction and occasional intervention are regarded as friendly. But what are the realities behind the benign portraits?

At the beginning of a classroom day, Japanese children rise and bow, saying *Sensei, onegai shimasu*, "Teacher, please do us the favor [of teaching us]." This is more than a formal incantation of respect and humility. The Japanese word *sensei* (teacher) has much deeper resonance than its English equivalent, even when the latter is capitalized as a form of address. "Hey, Teach" has no equivalent in Japanese.

In East Asian tradition, teaching is a respected profession, a lifetime commitment, a much sought after occupation. Accordingly, some Japanese critics repeatedly trot out the presumably negative effects of contemporary education on the role of the teacher and look back nostalgically at prewar or even Meiji-period schools. But compared to counterparts in other developed societies, the Japanese teacher has an enviable role and job.

Because learning and the ensuing academic credentials are the most valued pursuits and goals in contemporary Japanese life, teachers are still greatly valued. However, their role has changed subtly since prewar times. The prewar teacher was himself actively revered as the embodiment of virtue; the concrete knowledge the child might absorb was secondary to the moral virtue acquired by emulating the teacher. In the modern case, the teacher is not a holy guru, but a conveyor of information and a way for the child to engage himself in the pursuit of learning. It used to be that mastering the material had value because it came from a revered teacher; now the teacher has value because he imparts specific knowledge.

The pre-modern teacher usually taught in a *terakoya,* as we learned earlier. Having no particular training, he was often a person who had retired from another occupation. Classes were diverse in age and ability, and teachers often gave individual attention and assignments, as was the case in an American nineteenth-century one-room schoolhouse. Recitation was a common form of participation, especially where a community could not afford books or writing boards for all students. Memorization through recitation was also itself valued as evidence of a child's ability to concentrate. In general, the quality of oral performance was stressed. Hence group recitation and reliance on memory, born in necessity, were not evidence of rigid group discipline and authoritarian values, though the harmony represented by the unity of voices was valued. Texts were Confucian, sometimes Buddhist; arithmetic was basic, and other subject matter unstandardized. Texts were used not only as a way to teach reading, but more importantly, as the bearers of explicit personal and social morality, just as virtue was embodied in the teacher himself.

Teaching became standardized and bureaucratized during the Meiji period, when universal schooling was introduced by national authorities. At first the teaching force was diverse: *terakoya* instructors, former priests, a few housewives, and the younger "new teachers" trained at normal schools. Gradually the latter became ascendant. As elsewhere, women began to fill the ranks of teachers in elementary schools, but the upper levels were dominated by male teachers. Even today women are only 15 percent of high school teachers in Japan, compared to 50 percent in the United States.

THE TEACHER AND THE JOB

Those who choose teaching as a career tend to be middle or lower middle class in origin[1] and often come from smaller cities or rural areas. Depending on their generation, origin, and personal and political predilections, teachers see the job differently. Rohlen notes that younger teachers are beginning to regard it as an opportunity for creativity and independence, unlike the life of the bureaucratized "salaryman." Rohlen also points out that independence must be perceived as relative, and that teaching in Japan would seem to an American to be an intensely group-centered profession.[2] Compared to other ways of making a living, however, teaching in Japan does allow a certain measure of autonomy, and the teacher, for the most part, is free to avoid the after-work group socializing which is nearly compulsory in large organizations.

What may be the most striking and enviable aspect of the life of the Japanese teacher is that he earns a relatively good living. Elementary and junior high school teachers' starting salaries average $19,000 per year, while high school teachers start at $20,000. Other Japanese public sector workers earn an average of $17,000, and teachers begin professional life on pretty much a par with college graduates entering the corporate world. As is customary in Japan, pay increases are tied to seniority. Of course, after fifteen years, the corporate worker who has risen on a ladder enjoys higher income than the teacher, but the differential is very much less than that in the United States. The starting salary for an American teacher, averaging $17,600, is less than that of any other group of college graduates, and rises after fifteen years to only $25,000, half that of his college classmates in other professions at the same career stage.

While the sacredness of teaching and the self-sacrifice involved in the traditional model of the teacher's life have been modified by current practice and ideology, elements of the traditional remain. A teacher visits the families of each of his students at least once a year—now officially part of a pedagogical rationale which has it that a teacher can understand a pupil better if his family life is known. Furthermore, students visit their teachers, and especially beloved former teachers, at their homes during the New Year's holidays.

Even a university professor engages in a nurturant intimacy with his students, an intimacy that transcends subject matter and methods of the lecture hall. Many take their students—the inner circle of disciples—on yearly retreats to the countryside. One professor reported that even he was astounded at how maternal his role was expected to be with young adults. On his expedition to an inn with six of his graduate students, he was awakened in the middle of the night by a call from a student at his door: *Sensei, naka ga suita,* "Teacher, I'm hungry."

How Teachers Define Themselves

The range of identities in teaching has been polarized by the contrapuntal dialogue between the Japan Teachers' Union and the ministry of education. One of the chief points of controversy is the definition of the job. But the issue goes beyond the polarity of teacher-as-worker versus teacher-as-exploited-and-devoted-servant. Singleton surveyed middle-school teachers on work titles of preference and found variance in how they would like to define their role.[3] This ranges from traditional *sensei* to *rodosha* (laborer or worker). Cummings cites a study made in the Kansai area, dominated by the rather radical Teachers' Union, which shows that 83.7 percent of teachers here prefer to be called workers.[4] The connotations include a well-defined limit to work hours, extensive benefits, a dedication to equality of education for all children, active participation in decision making, and, of course, solidarity with fellow-teachers in other schools. Other terms of self-identity include: *kyoin* (more bureaucratic than *sensei*, meaning a member of a school's teaching staff), *kenkyusha* (meaning, generally, a researcher), and *gakusha* (meaning scholar, or in the Chinese sense, a moral exemplar).

THE TRAINING OF TEACHERS

Because a teaching career is highly desired, to receive job training in the best programs is very competitive. Even though 86 percent of Japanese institutions of higher learning have teacher-education programs, they can admit only one-quarter of the applicants. In the end, about 30 percent of college graduates in Japan acquire teaching credentials.

Requisites for certification include a standard liberal arts program and courses in professional education and teaching-field specialization. The latter include principles of education, educational psychology, methods, and a student-teaching internship of two to four weeks. Though expectations and standards are high, there is little monitoring of the teacher preparation programs, which are self-monitored through consensus, like much in Japanese education, giving the appearance (to a Westerner) of more centralized control than exists.

Once hired, a teacher of whatever self-definition has a well-defined track to follow and predictable options for promotion. The first years are considered an apprenticeship, and as in other jobs, the teacher's and the school's investment in training is seen to pay off for both under a "permanent employment system." In prewar Japan a novice teacher would be explicitly matched with a senior teacher, and through intensive interaction there would develop a close bond by which the lore and practices of the profession would be imparted. A common practice was to have teachers serve as night guards for schools, and by custom a veteran teacher would be teamed with an apprentice to patrol the school together. During these quiet hours, the bonding and exchange took place that shaped the training of the younger teacher. With more bureaucratized training and union-led restriction of teachers' work hours after the war, the practice died out, but schools still attempt to match junior with senior teachers at least for the first year. Also, two or three times a month, the new recruits in a school meet as a group with the principal and veteran teachers to discuss experiences and receive advice. This experience-hierarchy is constantly invoked. New or weaker teachers are seen to need support, and do not have to rely on a "sink or swim" philosophy. All teachers know that they can lean on others and (usually without shame) approach their seniors for help.

There is another important reason why schools must support their teachers. Japanese teachers will say that the school has a responsibility to provide a good education for each and every child. And because children and their parents cannot select their teachers, but are assigned to a class, the school feels it owes them a good teacher. Hence the egalitarian emphasis in Japanese education, at least ideally, prevents a child from getting a bad education because of a bad teacher.

Japanese teachers' performances are monitored carefully and teachers work together to improve their skills. This is done through weekly grade level meetings in which all the teachers of the same grade meet to discuss the study plan for the coming week and any problems or issues that have come up in class. They also have daily contact with each other, in the teachers' room, where the desks of teachers of the same grade are clustered together. Thus the experience of children of the same level in different classes is remarkably consistent, with the skills of the veteran teachers benefiting more than their own charges.

Transfer patterns affect the quality of teaching in schools. Within a school district, teachers can be moved around depending on the needs of particular schools; an effort is therefore made to balance the resources of all. Teachers can be given as little as two months' notice before a transfer. Yet early and frequent transfers are not often regarded as bad for the career of an ambitious teacher. In fact, for those who want to become school administrators, there are well-understood paths of promotion involving many postings early in their careers. Such teachers will work first in schools in less desirable areas, urban or rural, and will spend a few years of seasoning or rustication as a proof of dedication. These teachers will move frequently in their first ten or fifteen years, often leaving their families behind. If they prove their mettle, they will eventually become school principals in their later years, having exhibited the qualities necessary for success in any Japanese organization: personal ability, self-sacrifice, and dedicated patience.

A Teacher's Day

Shimizu-sensei, age thirty-two, has taught for ten years in elementary school. He and his wife and two children live in a western suburb of Tokyo, not far from the school where he teaches sixth grade. Having graduated from Meiji University in Tokyo, where he majored in biology, he took an extra year for teacher-training courses. His wife is a teacher too, but took three years off after the birth of their second child. She wants to return to teaching kindergarten when her younger child enters kindergarten in another year and a half. For the present, because they are living on one income, Shimizu has taken on private tutoring jobs in the evenings.

Shimizu's day is very crowded. Although his hours of classroom instruction are relatively short—about fifteen hours per week compared to twenty-five hours per week in the United States—he has many other duties that keep him busy during the entire school day until nearly six in the evening.

When he arrives for the day around 7:30 a.m., he goes directly to the teachers' room, leaves off his lesson preparations, and makes copies of materials for his students. All teachers are present at what is a morning convocation of the school, then attend teachers' meetings from 8:15 to 8:35, and join their homeroom classes. Shimizu's class is designated 6–3, one of about forty students. The students are fairly homogeneous in background, from white-collar nuclear families consisting of husband, wife, and children. Only a third of the families have a grandparent living with them. Shimizu knows something of each family, for this is his third year with almost all of the children.

The morning begins briskly with a class meeting, followed by a math class, then a Japanese-language class and recess before a double-period science class. The children stay in the homeroom for the first two classes but move to the laboratory for science. Thus the transition between subjects is relatively smooth, the teacher not having to wait for or be interrupted by stragglers coming in late. The thundering herds of students in the halls, watched over by "hall monitors," which punctuate the American school day are not part of the Japanese educational experience.

Shimizu's classroom is next to 6–1 and across the hall from 6–2, leaving all the sixth graders and their teachers in close proximity. This geographical clustering by grade creates what Rohlen has called a "neighborhood," acting, as traditional neighborhoods do in Japan, to keep order and maintain high standards by mutual observation and peer pressure. This is explicitly invoked by teachers, who create a mood of friendly competition and comparison between the behavior, tidiness, and other attributes of their own class and those adjoining.

During the science class, which is taught by another teacher, Shimizu returns to the teachers' room. Sometimes he accompanies his group to the more specialized classes and sits in the back of the room to observe his students' work. Today, however, he is busy with additional preparations for the weekly schoolwide faculty meeting. He is responsible for presenting a statement on the progress of the entire sixth grade, and is concerned about how his charges will move on to junior high school.

Lunch is served in the classroom. The four sixth graders whose task it is to serve it have donned their white smocks and caps, and trundle a lunch cart down the hall. The other children, meanwhile, take out their own pocket handkerchiefs and spread them on their desks. Shimizu does the same, at his desk, eating the day's chicken and vegetables, bread and milk and fruit. Like the children, he cleans up after himself.

The afternoon has a different pace. It is Shimizu's turn to help monitor recess after lunch. Then the class returns for social studies and music, before splitting into two groups for domestic science and shop classes. A final half-hour for class meeting ends the school day. Shimizu, however, stays on for the two-hour faculty meeting and only at six is ready to go home, with papers to correct and lesson plans to prepare.

He has several other mental burdens to accompany him. He knows that a P-TA meeting is coming up. Here he'll see the parents, at least the mothers, of his students. He is worried about the performances of two of them, and needs to confer privately with the parents before the meeting. He is also worried about his relationship with one of the other sixth grade teachers, who has subtly criticized him for a friendship with the principal, an old family connection. Shimizu, like his colleague, is a member of the Japan Teachers' Union but is not as active as his colleague in political discussions; nor is he as overtly opposed to school administrators. He is very tense in faculty and grade meetings because he feels that at any time the private disagreement may be publicly displayed—under some other guise of course. Shimizu finds it hard to reconcile his own feelings of commitment to the school as a whole with his political inclination to support teachers as a separate constituency within the school.

Mostly, however, his big problem is the parents who have asked him to employ more rigid discipline in the classroom; to be tougher with their children, who they do not feel are studying hard enough. His own predilection is a traditional one: commanding respect within a friendly and relaxed environment. The children know he cares for them but won't take any nonsense. Shimizu doesn't think that informality is incompatible with politeness and deference; he feels that he can responsibly develop proper study habits and human relationships within the class *and* maintain proper distance between himself and his students without losing the intimacy that he sees as a means and goal of good teaching.

He's glad that he teaches elementary school and not middle or high school, where pressure from parents is even greater. Like Sagara, who teaches the *juku* described later, Shimizu feels that there has been a serious distortion of the methods and outcomes of teaching in secondary schools. And while the pay and status of high school teaching are somewhat greater than his own, he has chosen to work with younger children, upon whom the pressure of entrance examinations weighs less heavily.

As an elementary school teacher, Shimizu can concentrate on his set of relationships with his class and on learning itself, rather than on an individual child's rank and progress up the achievement ladder. Although some parents may hound him to become more of a taskmaster, he is on the whole undisturbed by *kyoiku mamas*. Consequently, he has more time for his family and for himself than do his friends who are secondary school teachers; unlike them, he can sometimes take a Sunday off to pursue his hobbies. An expert fly caster, he also enjoys watercolor painting—interests he sometimes combines with day trips to the countryside.

PROBLEMS AND PERSPECTIVES

Teaching in Japan is not what it was, if it ever was the sacred and revered profession to which sentiment and Confucian ideology refer. In any case, the modern classroom is not always a harmonious place; teachers are subject to a range of conflicting pressures from school authorities, peers, parents, and children. Meanwhile, the job of teaching itself is in flux as teachers explore a variety of identities and roles. They also find themselves at the center of debates on school reform, buffeted by constituencies and lobbyists from opposing political and ideological positions.

Teachers, influenced by their experiences and by the public media, say that their central concern is the physical safety of themselves and their students. Some, particularly in middle schools, worry that they might be attacked by a child or children. Others worry that their students may be the victims of bullying by others. And all of them worry about their responsibility to the students, to parents, and to the school in extreme circumstances.

Subtler negative moods, brought on by jealousy and competition, impede the process by which Japanese children learn. And their teachers resent it, because they think the bad feeling is imposed by external realities outside their control. On all these issues, generational differences exist.

Nevertheless, Japanese teachers, by and large, have a favorable environment in which to work, especially when compared to their counterparts in the West. The pressures induced by the entrance examinations and by parents trying to better their own children's chances in the competitive struggle are offset to a considerable extent by the support teachers receive from each other, from the schools, and from the union. Furthermore, and most important if one takes a comparative view, teachers have the support of the sociocultural consensus that education really matters; and while this broadly based accord will not protect a teacher from physical attack in the classroom, the consensus does ensure that the incidence of such attacks is quite rare.

One might set the view of a teacher's life in Japan against the view of the lives of old people. For both, tradition emphasizes respect, reverence, and support from both family and community. Recently, however, the lives of the aged (especially those who cannot live within extended families) have been shown to be less than "golden," just as teachers have been regarded as being under siege. Both have suffered, it seems, from the erosion of traditional values. However, the aged who have fallen through the cracks in Western societies might still envy the old people of Japan, who have only in statistically rare cases been abandoned. Similarly, most Western teachers would probably prefer the generally well socialized Japanese child and the predictable, rewarding career of the Japanese teacher over what they now have.

PART II

THE EXPERIENCES OF CHILDHOOD

6

LEARNING AT MOTHER'S KNEE

Japanese mothers and teachers both rely on sensitivity, intimacy, and shared goals as the means by which they can shape a child's growth. The closeness, physical and psychological, of the relationship with a child is the measure of the success of Japanese mothering. Close physical proximity gives the mother a chance to develop an intuitive understanding of her child's character, behavior, and feelings—an understanding that she uses to shape the child's development. One of my students, who has a Japanese mother, wrote a paper describing his relationship with her. His epigraph for the paper is a poem:

> I am
> like the clay
> always being molded
> into different shapes
> by two firm hands

The Japanese mother intuits the desires and needs of the child's inner self and fulfills them without expecting the child to verbalize his own. She responds to his unexpressed signals and encourages his reading of her cues as well, thus creating an atmosphere of mutual sensitivity to mood and subtle body language. The child is thus constantly taught to avoid situations in which he causes trouble or discom-

95

fort for others (*meiwaku o kakeru*). This encourages the child to reflect upon the consequences of his actions for others, as well as to expect from them the same kind of consideration. In the end, Japanese child-rearing develops a sensitivity and inclination to respond to the subtle mood states of other people.[1]

Japanese mothers can "cooperate" in this way with their children without risking their own "authority" because, as Lanham has pointed out, they are "free of ego-based assertions of authority over their own children, even responding to their criticisms of their own behavior with ready apologies."[2]

Using her relationship with the child as a model, the mother trains the child in the ways of interpersonal relationships, but with the difference that between mother and child behavior is permitted that is nowhere else allowed. In other words, to develop in the child a need to be dependent, the capacity to reciprocate dependency, and an ability to read subtle emotional cues to others' moods is the mother's most important responsibility.

As she teaches, the mother attempts at all times to avoid open confrontation with the child. By constantly repeating her requests and showing enthusiasm and support for the child's successes, she encourages the child a step at a time down the path toward her goals for him. The expression *Haeba tate tateba ayumi no oyagokoro* (If he crawls, encourage him to stand; if he stands, have him walk—such is the parent's way) indicates the way goals are set by the mother. If the child rebels, she attempts to protect her relationship with him rather than forcing the issue at the expense of alienating him. In this way, as we saw earlier, she trains him not only to the style of interpersonal behavior valued by her and society at large, but also to the daily tasks (e.g., brushing his teeth or dressing himself) that he needs to be able to perform to become responsible for himself. Thus, the Japanese child is not confronted with a set of inflexible demands, but with constant suggestion and encouragement and an unworried expectation that he will eventually conform.

THE HOME CURRICULUM

To ensure that their children receive the grounding for successful school careers, most mothers train the child in school-related activities during the preschool years. The gradual shift in emphasis from the mother's role in fostering "good breeding" (*shitsuke*) to an emphasis on home training to prepare for school (*yoji kyoiku*) occurs around the age of three. Teachers do not encourage the training that goes on at home, but most middle-class mothers continue the practice. Most mothers in urban areas teach their preschool children to read and write the phonetic alphabet, and most children can count to one hundred and work simple computational problems involving amounts under ten before they reach first grade. They can also sing or recite several songs and poems. Most preschools do not teach these abilities systematically, and it is largely due to the efforts of the mother that the child develops the skills before he enters first grade.

What do Japanese mothers do in the home to teach their children? What do they do to foster cognitive development, in particular, since that is what interests Americans who envy Japanese test scores? The data on mothers' use of teaching aids, on hours spent teaching a child to read, write, compute, and do other educational activities of the kind we would recognize, is very impressive.

Japanese mothers take the education of preschoolers at home very seriously indeed, providing a curriculum that is consciously and sensitively managed. But most of the activities are informal. Mothers spend many hours in cooperative games and pursuits with their children, such as drawing, reading storybooks, and playing writing and counting games. Parents also buy many supplementary aids and materials such as workbooks and children's magazines. Even at the playground, where an American mother usually spends her time monitoring a child's physical safety and his social interactions, the Japanese mother uses the time to teach: "How many stones does Taroo have? Let's take one away. . . ." The Japanese mother's didactic interventions usually involve activities through which she can engage herself with the child, while American mothers are more likely to buy games and toys advertised as providing "hours of happy and educational independent activity."

Besides increasing a child's store of information and cognitive skills, the mother tries to train the child to concentrate. The importance of single-minded effort, of intense dedication, is very clearly imparted to the child. The mother keeps the youngster doing only one thing at a time; everything else is left aside. In Japan some teenagers are called *nagarazoku:* members of the "tribe of 'whilers' "—doing one thing while doing something else. This mothers discourage ardently. They even feel that when their children are watching TV, *they should do that and nothing else.*

A program of intensive learning at an early age is a fully conscious strategy on the part of the mother to improve her child's chances in competitive examinations to come. But what fuels her energetic efforts is not finally a drive for advantage: rather, it is her desire to engage her child actively, and the cognitive content of that activity is simply the current vehicle for that engagement. Of course, she realizes that it might serve him well, but she also feels wholehearted pleasure in the interaction through which the advantage is being developed.

THE MOTIVATING BOND

The psychodynamics by which the mother carries out her awesome responsibilities hinge upon the development of an emotional closeness between the mother and child. To form the bond, the child needs the mother as the object of his seeking for indulgence (*amae*), which she has encouraged. By indulging the child and by explicitly training him in the distinction between behavior appropriate to such an "indulged" relationship and that appropriate to the outside world, the mother preserves the intimacy of the mother–child relationship and reinforces the necessity for "social graces" in dealings beyond the family. At the same time, she gauges her demands for more mature behavior on the child's part to his ability to meet expectations. By showing that she is hurt when the child refuses to fulfill her reasonable demands, she implicitly threatens to withdraw affection. In the end, the mother gradually shapes the child's behavior toward greater maturity. If the child flatly refuses to go along, she typically backs down, and while displaying hurt, reaffirms the emotional bond with the child. However, she will continue to look for the opportune time to reassert her desires, confident that through her understanding of the child's inner self, she will finally triumph.

Although this description of the mother's manipulation of the relationship's psychodynamics makes her appear extremely Machiavellian, most Japanese mothers are not overtly conscious of their psychological methods, and do not feel that there is anything underhanded about them. On the contrary, they feel that what they do naturally supports the child. Moreover, what we might call manipulation is seen as completely appropriate management of the child, who is in any case not seen as an independent unit. What the mother is "managing" is a relationship, not a person. Outside observers also feel that from a long-range perspective, the patient, child-focused socialization methods are probably less damaging or manipulative than techniques used in other cultures, including our own.

Throughout, the mother wants to prepare her child to succeed in the world outside the home—the child's success is her success. But she is concerned about much more than this. Early on, she wants to develop a relationship with her child that will last a lifetime. Accordingly, her long-term perspective on mothering very definitely takes into account not only present but future mutuality. By providing understanding, nurturance, and sensitivity to the child's needs, and by training the child to reciprocate, the Japanese mother finds herself within a relationship that she hopes will last until the day she dies.

LEARNING THE WAY

What other social and psychological skills does the mother encourage? For her, the "good" child is one who participates wholeheartedly in the pursuit of the adult's goals, who in fact has taken them on as his own. That wholeheartedness is at least as important as the success that may result from the child's internalizing adult objectives. In other words, the way in which a child does something is more the measure of the child's character than the outcome of what he does. American children tend to be judged by the latter.

In Japan at any age, one's attitude is integral to one's performance. Thus, any task is composed of appropriate attitude, energy, patience, and attention to detail. The priority of process over product is fully shown in traditional apprenticeships and the acquisition of certain traditional crafts and skills: if you learn how to do something very carefully, and pay exquisite attention to every step needed to make it, the finished product will naturally be a good one. As indicated in the popular book *Zen and the Art of Archery*,[3] all skill and art lie in preparing to loose the arrow. If this is done well, the archer needn't think about whether the arrow will fly true or not. Similarly, in the tea ceremony, in origami, in gardening, and in the construction of automobiles, understanding "the way" is more important than the "perfect" product itself. In short, the moral force of method is greater than quantifiable result. Thus, even small children are taught that you fold the paper "exactly so," you cut precisely along the line, you place your shoes exactly parallel and in just the right spot near the door.

What we see as compulsive, competitive "perfectionism" the Japanese see as a satisfying completion of a set of detailed tasks. When a Japanese child learns to do something, he is taught to do it in tiny steps, each one seen as very important and eminently doable. The mastery of one discrete step is greatly applauded, with the child experiencing a moment of clear accomplishment. Michael Kirst notes that "Japanese children are taught that each repetition of a process always contains something new. They learn to discriminate tiny variations in routines as they are repeated." He goes on to conclude that this "probably helps the Japanese perfect and improve new technology that other countries develop."[4] But in my view the Japanese trait means much more for child rearing and cognitive development than it does for economic development.

A Western therapist might consider Japanese behavior as so obsessed with control that it masks suppressed aggression. In fact, our lack of attention to detail, and the delay of gratification until the completion of a large task, provide us with less mundane, moment-to-moment satisfaction. This in turn keeps us feeling frustrated and incomplete, as we value only the final, sometimes unobtainable end product. We have talked earlier about the differences in the meaning of creativity in the two societies, which also have to do with how the two differently regard task completion. Suffice it to emphasize here that what counts, in a Japanese home and a Japanese school, is a child's commitment to work hard within a fully supportive ambience; what does not count are gifts or talents with which a youngster is endowed by God or nature. Thus, the mother's and teacher's most significant contribution to a child's future is a capacity to instill the importance of engagement, the same engagement they themselves show—positive, wholehearted, energetic commitment—while at work on a task to produce a result.

JOINING THE GROUP: THE USES OF PRESCHOOLS

If the environment of the home provides so much intensive learning, what is the place of nursery schools and other preschool forms of activity? Who uses them, and why? Masaru Ibuka, the head of the Sony Corporation, wrote a best-selling book, *Kindergarten Is Too Late,* in which he claimed that the most profitable time to engage a child in formal learning is the very earliest years. As a result, parents intensified a commitment to the cognitive development of their children, enrolling them in greater numbers in nursery schools and special programs and spending even more money on educational games and toys. Ibuka, like many teachers and educational policymakers, wanted parents to spend more time and energy educating the "whole child," making him more "well rounded," as Americans say. Instead, parents continue to regard formal schooling as absolutely essential to a child's future academic success, and go so far as to prepare not only their children but themselves for entrance examinations into the most highly rated preschools.

In a recent study conducted by the Nishinomiya Pre-School Education Study Group, preschool mothers were polled for their attitudes concerning preschool education. They were asked general questions on child rearing and learning, and on teaching and training in formal institutions. As for the answers, most mothers agreed with the proposition that a child's nature and character are not given at birth and that his development is externally influenced. They also felt that preschools should provide a safe environment for physical development and that cognitive learning is not to be emphasized—they wanted the school to stress socialization and deemphasize preparation for elementary school.

Furthermore, when asked what sort of teacher they preferred for their children, they ranked gentleness and caring first, then patience and liveliness (*akarui*). Less important were discipline, rigor, and technical knowledge.[5]

Preschools include *yochien* and *hoikuen* (nursery schools and daycare). The ministry of education reported in 1979 that 65 percent of five-year-olds, 50 percent of four-year-olds, and 7.5 percent of three-year-olds were enrolled in nursery school or kindergarten. Half of each percentage figure was probably enrolled in daycare, which meant five-year-olds' enrollment was close to 100 percent. Furthermore, the overall percentage of enrollment in either nursery school or daycare was 63.8 percent for three-, four-, and five-year-olds when averaged together. Moreover, from 1965 to 1979 the number of institutions serving preschool children had doubled to over 15,000 such schools serving almost 2.5 million children. Of these children, over 74 percent were enrolled in private preschools, which charge substantial tuition and other fees.[6]

Since preschool has become an almost universal experience for the Japanese child, its environment and characteristics have become a significant formative influence. What is a preschool like? In some important ways, it is like the child's home. First, some 96 percent of all preschool teachers are women. In general, the younger the pupil, the more likely his or her teacher is to be female. The atmosphere, as described by Catherine Lewis[7] and others, is warm and nurturant, basically nonacademic and play-oriented. In spite of parental desire to push cognitive development, most teachers devote themselves to the social and behavioral. Meanwhile, daycare teachers prefer to encourage children to tend to their own needs whenever possible.

Japanese teachers, according to Lewis, assume that children *want* to be good, which governs their management of the classroom. Bad behavior, in other words, stems from "not understanding" rather than willful misbehavior. In any case, children seem to comply voluntarily with a teacher's request, making defiance and insubordination rare. Children typically immerse themselves enthusiastically and responsibly in self-directed activity, exhibiting long periods of concentration, and soliciting and requiring little attention from teachers. And a single child's behavior is indulged even to the point where the entire group might be inconvenienced.

As previously mentioned, nursery schools (and kindergartens also) in no way encourage a mother's program for cognitive development. In fact, as observed by Lois Taniuchi,[8] schools prefer to regard the child as a blank slate, trainable in the specific behavior and skills seen as appropriate to a specific educational environment. But like the mother, the school feels a child has no discernible preexisting abilities, and as a new recruit to school, he is raw material to be molded and formed by the teachers.

Every Japanese group or institution seems to feel the same way: to see any newcomer as totally malleable, carrying no identity-conferring baggage of skills or predispositions. Hence a bank trains its college-graduated new recruits as if they had had no training for their new jobs.[9] The bank, like all Japanese companies, tries to hire "generalists" who have studied no technical trade making them specialists. This means that a mid-career job changer must begin again at the bottom, to be "born again" in the new life the shift of group brings. In private life the practice is particularly telling for a new bride, who enters her husband's family to be trained "from scratch" in the methods and habits of the new group. The *kafu,* or "ways of the house," are seen to be completely unique—the way grandmother makes pickles, the schedules and rituals of the day. By extension, the school is a new family, having both the child's best interests at heart and representing a whole world of new expectations.

What does the small child as new recruit learn in his new life? What is considered important, whether in kindergarten or the early years of elementary school, is not drastically different from what is valued at home. But the context is quite different: instead of learning through the mother's persuasive, engaged, and constant attention, the child at school learns through more impersonal, though still engaged, direction. So the first lesson learned is that he is only one child among many, and that the others must be attended to as well. This is not so different, of course, from the same lesson learned during the early years in American schools, but the Japanese message goes much further. In Japan not only does one wait one's turn for highly valued personal attention, but one also learns that there are clear rewards for being attentive to other people and sensitive to their ideas and concerns. In other words, "getting along with others" is not just a means for keeping the peace in the classroom but something which is a valued end in itself.

The second lesson learned, early on, is that there is a right way to do things and that it is worth all the time it takes to get to know that way. Slowly teachers encourage children to listen and concentrate, as a first step toward doing things the right way. Similarly, other school customs and habits are inculcated quietly, with attention paid to "the way we do it."

Nursery school is not regarded, at least by teachers, as the first step on the road to the entrance examination. Integrating oneself into the life of the group, emotional sensitivity to others, and learning the right way to do something are the important lessons. The stated goals, which are typical, of Sakuranbo Nursery School in Saitama-ken are to raise children full of sensitivities, competence, physical strength, sympathy with friends, and the capacity to respond well in various environments. At Sakuranbo four-year-old children built a rabbit hutch together as a long-term project, but they first went to a zoo to observe rabbits in hutches, then made drawings and developed a model, and finally built the actual hutch. The school says that children "need the confidence they can derive from cooperation."

Japanese teachers strongly believe, and act on the belief, that the "group life" of the class is the entirely natural outcome of children's predilections to play together, to become friends. And so they say, as Catherine Lewis and Lois Taniuchi Peak report,[10] that children who don't feel that group activities are "more fun" than individual ones don't yet "know the happiness of playing together."

Turning to American middle-class mothers, what do they want from a nursery school? Usually they would like it to provide cognitive enhancement for the child or free time for themselves, or both. Neither of these is given as an explicit reason by Japanese mothers. Why, then, do their children attend? Some, of course, are sent because the school, even though it provides no explicit academic training, does provide the illusion that children enrolled have an advantage in the race to college. Yet a recent survey showed that even private kindergartens, widely thought to provide accelerated academic programs, do very little to push cognitive development. In fact, only 13 percent of the elite kindergartens help children to develop an acquaintance with a few written characters, and only 8 percent provide any work with numbers. Public kindergartens offer no training at all in reading or counting. Teachers say that they like to inspire interest in reading and computation but do not like to teach either. And they don't.

There are, however, preschool *juku* that explicitly try to impart academic skills to help the children pass tests to get into private kindergartens and elementary schools. The attendance at these schools is limited to a very small part of the urban population. During the preschool years, most urban middle class children do receive *some* sort of private instruction besides the preschool. But this is not usually given over to academic subjects and the choices here are often influenced by fads (music lessons, drawing and painting, swimming, and English are currently popular). In any case, the purpose is basically enrichment.

In one type of preschool, the daycare center, the schedule is usually arranged for the convenience of working mothers. Yet some mothers who do not work prefer to send their children to daycare centers, even though admission preference is given to children of working mothers. These nonworking mothers say they like the emphasis placed on self-reliance within an atmosphere less achievement-oriented. There are also working mothers who send their children to nursery schools despite problems with the schedule and pressure on the mother's time. In general, both nursery schools and daycare centers are play-oriented, though the former usually draw pupils from a slightly higher socioeconomic group. Accordingly, the nursery school implies "an advantage."

If the home is an indulgent environment, it is no wonder that Japanese parents feel that social and other training must take place outside it. We already know about the pre-modern tradition of sending children to be apprenticed in another family's household, because the child, the Japanese believe, can be better trained in a home not his own, or at least away from the tolerance of mothers and grandmothers like Masa's. This was particularly true among families practicing the crafts and trades, when the child was heir to the family business. This custom seems to belie the Japanese principle that the only useful forms of knowledge are those acquired within the environment where they are used and applied. In this case it seems that the threat to learning from an overindulgent intimacy is stronger than the need to train someone to the practices of a particular socioeconomic unit.

But in general for the Japanese there is, as we have seen, a complementarity and not a contradiction between the social and emotional conditioning of training at home and training in the school and other environments. To see how this merging occurs, let's now look at a day in the life of a three-year-old Japanese boy.

KENICHI'S DAY

Kenichi is three and lives in Senri New Town near Osaka. He has a ten-month-old baby sister, and his father, Ryusuke Watanabe, is a lower-level manager in an electronics company. Ryusuke graduated from Osaka University, and Kenichi's mother, Keiko, from a junior college for women in Kobe. They live in what is known as a "2DLK" (two rooms plus dining/living/kitchen area) apartment in a large *danchi*, or "apartment complex" which has two eight-mat rooms (rooms are measured by the number of three-by-six-foot tatami mats making up the floor), a large kitchen with dining area, a bath, and a toilet room. One of the tatami rooms is the living area by day and the parents' sleeping area by night, the low table and pillows being stowed away and the *futon*s being laid on the matting. The baby sleeps with the parents. The other room is also all-purpose, and usually Kenichi sleeps there, in a child's bed. The room has been carpeted in Western style and the bed is Western also. His toys are everywhere, spilling out into all the other rooms. Sleeping arrangements are far from fixed, and often the mother moves her *futon* into Kenichi's area with the baby, especially when Ryusuke sleeps late or when one of the children is ill.

The apartment is on the fifth floor, and there is a community playground in the open area between Kenichi's building and the next one. The entire neighborhood apartment complex is relatively new, with various shops providing all basic necessities within a five-minute walk. Buses also pass nearby to take residents to Osaka and to the major shopping areas of Senri. The Watanabes hope someday to own their own single-family house and have a savings account for the purpose, into which they put as much as they can of Ryusuke's twice-a-year bonuses and anything else they can squirrel away. They know that the money for the house may be depleted or reduced by expenses they may incur for their children's education.

Kenichi's day begins with his sister's cries to be fed and changed. Kenichi himself burrows under the quilt and tries not to wake up, but finally rouses himself. It is a spring day, in early March, and he is to visit his new nursery school with his mother and sister. The school year begins in April in Japan and ends in March, and so now young children like Kenichi are being gradually introduced to their new life as school-goers. He isn't sure how he feels about the idea, and reassures himself by remembering that today will be just a visit and his mother has promised not to leave him there. He is excited by the prospect of being "a big boy."

His mother is already up, and has laid out a bowl of cereal, a glass of milk, and a piece of toast and butter for him. He is too excited to eat, and his mother yields—and adds chocolate to his milk to ensure that he takes something. He watches a cartoon on television while his mother bustles about tending to the baby, putting away the *futon,* making his bed, cleaning the dishes, and generally tidying up. All this time, his father has been eating breakfast and quietly getting ready to go to work, not much involved in the early-morning routine of the rest of the family. He leaves, after telling Kenichi that he should be proud of being "a big boy" and going to school, and that he hopes he will be good.

With the baby strapped to her back and with Kenichi at one hand, Keiko leaves the house and walks through the streets until they reach a small, one-story building made of cement blocks and surrounded by a fenced-in play yard. Other mothers and children are converging on the scene, most looking tentative or even anxious. But a few clearly are veterans of the process, and they are more relaxed, arriving just at the appointed hour.

Kenichi begins to clutch more tightly at his mother's hand and grabs her leg as well, trying to pull her away from the school. A few other children are crying and one is even lying on the ground, kicking and screaming. Mothers pull out candies, toys, whatever might divert the children, and bring out the moistened towels they always carry to tidy up disheveled offspring.

Kenichi is fascinated by one little boy who has begun to hit his mother furiously, and he forgets his own fears watching the tantrum. Just then the head of the school comes to the doorway to invite everyone to come in. Mothers and children enter.

The head of the school then greets the assembled newcomers, and, paying no attention to the miserable cries of some of the children, speaks of the happy times to come, and of the love the teachers already have for their new charges. She admonishes parents to be sure to prepare the children for the experiences of school, and to be extremely careful traversing the crowded city streets. She tells them that the goal of the school is to provide children with a cheerful and cooperative group experience, and that parents should not expect this to be the first step toward entrance to a prestigious university. She reminds them that children need support and that they are too young to be pressured by the future. She hopes that parents and teachers will be able to work together to provide a good environment for their children's happiness.

The children are then seated in a circle—at least those who can be lured away from their mothers. Some of the mothers join the circle, sitting just behind their children to encourage them to participate. For many of them, this is the first time they have experienced organized play with other children. Earlier age mates engage only in ''parallel play'' or simply observe each other from a distance at a playground. The principal introduces all children to the teachers, who begin a clapping hands game. They chant a simple song, and ask the children to sing too. The teachers then tell the children about all the activities they have planned, and show them the rooms, the washing and toileting facilities, and the collection of toys and materials. Then the teachers hand out snacks—juice and crackers—and while the children are eating, the parents begin to loosen up and talk with each other. After that, it is time to go home, and by now almost all the children want more school. Some begin to cry because they do not want to leave.

On the way home, Keiko feels like celebrating and takes Kenichi to an ice-cream store. She buys three ice creams on sticks. After these are eaten, they go to the park and let the baby play in the sandbox. Keiko feels relieved that Kenichi did not seem to mind school terribly, and yet she also wants him to know that she is still the one who indulges him with treats.

Kenichi tells a child he meets on the way home that he has just gone to school, and the child, a little older, mocks him and tells him he's only visited nursery school, not *real* school. With the wind knocked out of his sails a little, Kenichi begins to whine a bit and wants to be carried. His mother half-drags him home, and after feeding the baby and putting her down for a nap, she reads to Kenichi and then prepares lunch. Then, after Kenichi's nap, his mother takes the two children shopping for groceries and allows them to play in the apartment playground for a long time. Kenichi appears to have forgotten all about school. But when the next morning at breakfast his father asks what happened, Kenichi swells with pride and proceeds to narrate a very long winded version of the previous day's sixty-minute episode, with special attention given to the tantrums of the other children.

There are several things to point to here. First is the centrality of the mother in the child's life. We rarely see the father at all, and he rarely sees Kenichi awake. He is home on Sundays, and that day is usually "family day." A popular children's book treating the relationship of father and child is called *Nichiyoobi no Tomodachi* (My Sunday Friend). On Sundays the family may go together to a park or zoo, or go shopping in the large downtown department stores—if the father isn't sleeping off an exhausting week or playing compulsory golf with a client or superior. Time spent with one's family is sometimes ironically referred to as "family service" (in English) by some men.

The second aspect of the Watanabes' life to be noted is the isolation of the mother with her children. Keiko lives in a very large apartment complex and knows her neighbors only slightly. There are several families from her husband's company in the building, but an occupational connection does not bring the wives together; on the contrary, because of problems from jealousy and indiscreet revelations potentially harming the husbands' relations at work, the women whose husbands work together tend to politely avoid each other. Keiko has become friendly with some other mothers in the playground, but their children play together only there, and members of the age group rarely visit each other at home, with or without their mothers.

The adults to whom Keiko speaks regularly number only a few: the fish store lady and the vegetable seller, and the people who come to her door to sell magazines ("to enhance your child's chances in school") and birth control devices (most condoms are sold this way, to wives). Keiko does talk on the telephone a lot, to her sister, her mother, and sometimes an old school friend who lives on the other side of Osaka. In general, though, her daily relationships are confined to her children.

Another feature of life is the predictability of the day's events. While Keiko doesn't rigidly schedule them, and maintains a rather leisurely pace, her tasks are regular and her geographical arena rather constrained. There is not much of what an American middle-class mother would call outside "stimulus" in the child's day.

The school orientation visit itself was also rather unstimulating, and its very occurrence is regarded as enough to acquaint the child with the idea of school. The meeting was short, the messages were simple. In fact, the brevity of the session was intended to whet the child's appetite. This is very similar to the enticements programmed into the Suzuki violin teaching method,[11] in which the child is initially not allowed to handle the violin, but simply watches others play; when he finally is allowed to try his hand, he is given the instrument only for a very short time, leaving him wanting more.

Finally, one must note the positive tone that suffuses all the interactions with children. Rarely does one hear threats, warnings, or pronouncements, not to speak of character denunciations; nor do teachers or parents confront children directly. Over the sound of crying children, the principal tells them what a happy day it is, while mothers cajole and persuade through love, not war. Direct punishment is rare: mothers and teachers express displeasure in subtle, oblique ways (by American standards) and work strenuously to create an environment in which the child cannot help but wholeheartedly comply.

The approach here, which Americans might see as a sophisticated version of "behavior modification," is tied to more traditional practices. There is the story about the goal of Zen training. A disciple, it seems, has achieved mastery when he can keep a bird from flying off his arm simply by giving way every time the bird attempts to take off. Without resistance, the bird can get no purchase on the arm and cannot fly away. By analogy, the child is always on the arm of the teacher, whose "passivity" prevents him from rebelling. While we cannot believe that mothers and teachers never allow themselves to be angry, to punish openly, to express frustration with children, the model remains that of the mother with the newborn infant: to work toward merging rather than separating.

7

ELEMENTARY SCHOOLS

Harmony and Cooperation

When Kenichi is about to become a first-grader, his parents, teachers, school administrators, and the community at large will mobilize themselves to make his entrance into the world of "real school" a most significant moment in his life. The preparation, the ceremony, and the carefully organized techniques for involving him in all the activity and its symbolism contribute to the importance of the day. When the day comes, administrators, teachers, staff, parents, and Kenichi himself will over and over again express commitment to the school, to his classmates, and to his own growth.

Once again Kenichi will become a blank slate, just as he was as he entered nursery school and kindergarten—a candidate for initiation into another group. The socialization at home and preschool give him only a limited kind of "credential" rather than a set of recognized skills that he can display as his personal property.

Preparations for Kenichi's adjustment to school begin early. Again, he and his mother are invited to attend an orientation day, and perhaps make another visit as the beginning of school approaches. While children who have had older siblings in the same school often have more confidence, all of them approach the first day with a certain degree of anxiety. Mother has fussed over her son, bought new clothes (most public elementary schools do not have uniforms), equipped him with backpack and handkerchiefs, lunchbox and pencil case. Most schools will serve lunch, but some private schools and junior high schools rely on mothers to provide a well-balanced, aesthetic, and appealing lunch daily. (Teachers are known to send notes home to a mother whose lunch doesn't meet class standards.)

The first day parents and children arrive together at the school, which is usually within walking distance of the child's home, unless the child attends a private school and must be taken by bus or train. Parents and children, dressed to the hilt, converge on the schoolyard. Mothers wear their very best dresses, grandmothers come in kimono, and fathers wear the dark suits, white shirts, and polished black shoes which they may otherwise wear only to weddings and important company functions. The boys are in new dark suits with short pants and caps, the girls in new suits or party dresses and hats.

The ceremonies begin, with the whole school assembled to welcome the first-graders. The sixth-graders, the most senior in the school, act as big brothers and sisters to the first-graders, many of whom seem bewildered by all the novelty and attention. The older children pin name cards, with class assignments, on each first-grader. The principal of the school then welcomes everyone back, and offers some exhortatory and uplifting remarks to the students, parents, and teachers. Because his remarks are simple and not overdone, the audience takes his precepts to heart; parents and teachers will repeat some of his phrases to children in the days to come. The principal finishes with introductions of teachers and staff—including kitchen crew and maintenance people—and with a plea for caution while walking to school in traffic. Indeed, safety is one of the key responsibilities of the school, since it is school that has brought the children so far from their homes and through such perilous passage. Some words from sixth grade class leaders follow, as does introduction of the Parent-Teacher Association. The total effect of everything is a welcome into a new family, much vaster than the intimacy of the mother–child relationship but still caring and concerned. The school is always called "our" school.

Sixth-graders then accompany first-graders to their classrooms, and parents disperse or wait outside. The first day for first-graders is short, again only a taste of what is to come. The teacher gives them a brief welcome in the classroom and introduces them to its features and geography. She tells them that they will be working hard this year, but that they will also have fun. They are asked to respond to a roll call, by standing next to their desks and saying loudly and briskly "Present!" After a brief presentation of routines, materials, and plans, the teacher dismisses the class and the children wander back to their parents, who walk them home to change into play clothes and relax.

DETAIL AND PROCESS

When the year starts in earnest, the next day, the teacher does not wade directly into reading and computation or other academic subjects. She considers it far more important to socialize the children to the practices of group life and to the customs of this school.[1] She spends a very long time on such things as where one puts one's outdoor shoes, how one sits down and stands up, how one speaks in class, how one prepares one's desk for work (pencils at the top, notebook on the right, text on the left, etc.). As an American teacher knows, there are always some children for whom such things are difficult, and the girls tend to catch on early while some of the boys resist any routine.

One of the first lessons follows up on the first day's exhortation to speak up when roll is called. It is very important, children are told, to speak forthrightly and clearly in public, to project their voices and sound confident. The lesson here will stand them in good stead in school, work, and other situations to come.

This might seem paradoxical to a Westerner, who assumes that Japanese children are not encouraged to develop independent thought, speak their own minds, and project a strongly individualistic image to the world. Yet they are in fact, much more than our children, explicitly trained in public performance. This perhaps can be explained by separating *performance* as a skill, which anyone can learn, from responsibility for the content of one's own pronouncements. Once the distinction is made, the child is free to perform confidently since he is not usually displaying material of his own creation. So he isn't as vulnerable as a child who is asked to "state his mind." The quality of a Japanese child's performance is usually high but somewhat ritualized and predictable, thus perhaps minimizing risk to his ego. Later, of course, that same child does recite his own work, but by then he may well have justified confidence in his skill to perform.

Early on the similarly nonacademic lesson of self-reliance is also taught, which also may seem contrary to Western preconceptions of Japanese education. Self-reliance sounds to us like a big job for a first-grader, since it implies the prior development of a self with a set of independent motivations. We do of course push for independence among small children, but give them very little guidance about what this might mean and what they should do with it. So without clear domains for self-guided action, a Western child can find himself at sea, and later may lose the capacity for a truly independent, "creative" task. Meanwhile, the Japanese child is taught to master certain small, discrete, carefully delineated tasks, one at a time, and is given a long time to learn them. The teacher ensures that the approach has been learned well before the child is encouraged to go on. When he is, the child is then fully expected to be able to do *those tasks* self-reliantly. The goal of Japanese self-reliance is, finally, a capacity for self-motivated effort.

Japanese teachers are a very patient lot. Lessons are repeated as often as is necessary, and always in step-by-step fashion. The child is not expected to grasp a method or principle thoroughly at first, and doesn't feel any tension coming from high expectations. The teacher gives few overall explanations of the work at hand and many painstaking repetitions of small parts of the task or process. Moreover, verbal explanations are seen to get in the way of learning, though to an American teacher they may well come first. As a consequence of what is called "mastery learning," Japanese children often come up with the conceptual point underlying a lesson before the teacher has provided it.

By and large, American teachers are impatient with teaching of minute details, and may feel that more value or "prestige" comes from imparting an understanding of abstractions and an ability to verbalize the relationship between an abstract principle and the concrete instance at hand. Furthermore, American teachers often see any kind of emphasis on the rote learning of "unexplained" detail as leading a pupil to become too dependent on the instructor. In general, Western-ers feel that *principles* set the child's mind free, and want to release it for independent exploration as soon as possible. Japanese teachers, on the other hand, see pupil dependence as an important part of how one teaches, not in itself in any way infantilizing. And yet, as we shall soon see, "discovery learning" is also very significant in Japanese pedagogy.

ENERGY AND ENGAGEMENT

Because of our preconceptions of Japanese schooling, a walk into a typical fifth grade classroom in Japan may shock us. We might easily expect an environment suffused with rote learning and memorization, a structured and disciplined setting with an authoritarian teacher in control. This is far from the reality of most classrooms. Walking into a fifth grade math classroom, I was at first surprised: the mood was distinctly chaotic, with children calling out, moving spontaneously from their desks to huddled groups chatting and gesticulating. An American teacher would wonder "Who's in charge here?" and would be surprised to see the teacher at the side of the room, calmly checking papers or talking with some students. When I came to understand what all this meant, I realized that the noise and seeming chaos was in fact devoted to the work of the class; children were shouting out ideas for possible answers, suggesting methods, exclaiming excitedly over a solution, and *not,* as we might suppose, gossiping, teasing each other, or planning something for recess or after school. The teacher was not at all upset as long as total engagement in the appointed set of tasks persisted; she actually felt that the noise level was a measure of her success in inspiring the children to focus and work.[2]

Later the teacher presented the children with a general statement about the concept of cubing. But before any formulas or drawings were displayed, the teacher asked the class to take out their math diaries and spend a few minutes writing down their feelings and sense of anticipation about the new idea. Now, it is hard to imagine an American teacher beginning a lesson with an exhortation to examine one's emotional predispositions about cubing.

After this, the teacher asked for any conjecture from the children about the process and for some ideas about how to proceed. The teacher then asked the class to form *han* (working groups) of four or five children each, and gave out materials to work on. One group decided to build a cardboard model of a cubic meter and took materials into the hall to do it. In a while they returned, groaning under the bulk of what they had wrought, and there were gasps and shrieks as their classmates reacted to the size of the model and some tried to guess how many of them might fit inside. The teacher then outlined for the whole class a very difficult cubing problem, well over their heads, and gave them the rest of the class time to work on it. The class ended without a solution, but the teacher made no particular effort to get or give an answer, although she exhorted them to be energetic. It was several days before they came up with the answer; there was no deadline, but the excitement did not flag.

Several characteristics of the class deserve highlighting. First, priority was given to feelings, predispositions, and opportunities for discovery rather than providing facts and getting to an answer fast. The teacher emphasized process, engagement, and commitment rather than discipline (in our sense) and outcome.

Second, assignments were made to groups. (This, of course, is true at the workplace as well.) Individual progress and achievement are closely monitored, but children are supported, praised, and allowed scope for trial and error within the group. A group is also competitively pitted against other groups; a group's success is each person's triumph, and vice versa. Groups are made up by the teacher and are designed to include a mix of skill levels. The teacher helps the *hancho* (leader of a *han*) to choreograph the group's work, to encourage the slower members, and to act as a reporter to the class as a whole. The *hancho* is thus trained as an apprentice teacher as well, a job that falls to each child in turn.

TEACHER AND STUDENTS: MOTIVATION AND MANAGEMENT IN THE CLASSROOM

The pedagogies of a Japanese elementary school are based on the idea that all children are equal in potential, and that the excitement of learning can best be produced in a unity of equals. Teachers, especially those strongly influenced by the Teachers' Union, try to enforce this conviction and see themselves as stalwart defenders of the ethic of cooperation against the pressure exerted by a need to compete. For teachers, competition creates division and pulls a child toward a negative individualism. So the teacher uses group activity of various kinds to stem what he sees as a baleful threat, centrifugal and divisive, and resists singling out individual pupils except for short periods of time and in turn. To put it another way, the Japanese teacher wants to create and maintain a *kyoshitsu okoku,* or "classroom kingdom," of equals. His nurturant care surrounds the entire class, and can be graphically represented:

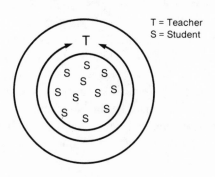

T = Teacher
S = Student

The need and desire for unity and harmony sometimes produces extreme strategems. In a school musicale, the recorders of children who don't play well are sealed with tape so that while these youngsters appear to be playing, no discordant sounds emerge to disrupt the smooth sound of class performance.[3] This sort of thing can be interpreted as unfortunate classroom public relations, but teachers feel that they are protecting the less able child from exposing inadequacy or "differentness." In general, a Japanese teacher will go to great lengths to protect a child from something he can't do very well.

A second model of classroom unity features a different view of the relationship of teacher to student. According to this model, the bonds which hold the group together are made up of the many dyadic relationships between the teacher and each student, as shown below:

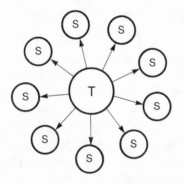

A more traditional model than the "classroom kingdom," this second model is the one employed by religious orders, artistic and craft schools, and other corporate organizations such as the prewar *zaibatsu* (holding companies) and academic departments in universities. The teacher here is presumed to skillfully manage all the individual relationships, knowing each student's strengths and weaknesses and attending to each individual's development. Most important, as the teacher relates to each student, he continues to stress the harmony of the whole, and he ardently tries to eliminate any sense of competition or alienation. This is the "vertical equality" model; and the other, an "equality of peers." Vertical equality is a way of teaching that demands much time and dedication. This means it is criticized by Teachers' Union supporters, who feel that the long hours of counseling and home visits required produce exploitation.

Japanese educators say that there is no evidence that one or another model produces greater academic success in the examinations. But many still believe that motivation for true learning can occur only in the second model, which they say has become hard to maintain in large classes.

Teachers often describe their work by telling the story of the cormorants, long-necked black birds that can be trained to dive for fish. Traditional cormorant fishermen owned flocks of such birds. Each bird was tied by a long cord held by the fisherman. If he had ten or fifteen birds, his handful of leashes would be hard to manage. While carefully keeping the leashes from tangling up, he had to handle each bird separately, even while minding the whole flock. This is the ideal classroom management mode: inducing harmony and paying close attention to the individual child.

The work team, or *han,* is used for both academic and nonacademic class purposes. It is, in fact, a part of pedagogical management, and its most common form is the *seikatsuhan,* or "daily life" *han.* For cleanup time, for lunch-serving time, for any other similar need, the unit of responsibility is the *han.* Teachers not only respect the didactic power of group learning, but also realize how appropriate it is for school activities of all kinds.

The *han* is also a teaching device used to engage children with diverse abilities in a single task. Though the group socializes children to see the value of cooperative teamwork, it also creates, teachers feel, an environment in which underachievers are stimulated to perform better, or at least feel fully included in what is going on. William Cummings talks about a socially backward boy put in a group with three "exceptionally tolerant" girls. They took him on as a "project," and "when he would not stand up for a class presentation, they would push him up, and when he struggled with an answer they would supply him with tips." Thus, Cummings says, "groups are conceived of as educational vehicles in the broadest sense rather than as mere instruments for rationalizing cognitive education."[4]

Unlike the teamwork of the *han,* American peer tutoring provides instruction devoted to individual rather than group needs. Not a way to make sure that everyone belongs, it is instead a way to reduce the problems some children have with the teacher–student authority relationship, permitting a more relaxed form of instruction. Learning is definitely not regarded as a group goal, and the usual form of peer tutoring is one-on-one. Since the teacher's authority carries no stigma and arouses no opposition in Japan, or rather, since authority per se engenders less anxiety than it does in the West, the Japanese seldom use it to motivate people. In the West, Esther Kohn says,[5] students need to feel control, or to feel that power can be shared, in order to feel self-esteem. In Japan, sharing power evinces the attainment of cooperation, which, I will say again, is itself a source of personal well-being.

Similarly, good human relationships are seen by Japanese teachers not only as means by which children can be taught various academic subjects but also as ends in themselves. So teachers try to watch friendships developing between children, and act as counselors to those who might be having trouble socially. Teachers know that children need to be appreciated and valued by other children, and that slow learners especially need peers to cheer them on. Friendships within the *han* are therefore regarded as developmentally important.

Most elementary school teachers say slow learners are few, especially in the early grades, but by the fourth grade there is more occasion to note problems. Here the "buddy system" of learning might be employed. Sometimes the parents of the faster learner will object, saying that to tutor another might slow down the learning of their own child. Teachers respond by asserting that not only is the role of the *oshiego,* or "teaching child," valuable for the learner, but the *oshiego* himself learns better through teaching. In any case, the faster learner usually finishes the classwork before the slower and has time on his hands, since Japanese schools have no accelerated program of any kind.

Besides the *han,* teachers use various physical arrangements of the classroom to facilitate learning. For some classes the desks, which are never fixed to the floor, are arranged facing front: when an experiment is to be conducted on the teacher's desk, slides are to be projected, or some other demonstration is to take place in the front of the room. At other times the desks may be arranged in groups of five or six, in the *hans* to which children have been assigned. For general class discussion, the teacher has the children move the desks into a U-shape, with the teacher's desk at the open end. The class may thus have as many as three different shapes during the same day, and preparing his or her study plan, a teacher indicates what the physical arrangement of the desks will be at what time.

Teachers also explicitly employ motivation techniques. One such is the concept of *donyu,* or "introduction," which means the initial moments of teaching a topic during which the children are "motivated to do the work actively." Consider the *seikatsu-tsuzurikata,* or "life composition," which has been around since well before World War II, especially in elementary schools. In a short essay, sometimes composed in a school diary, the child is encouraged to bring together what is learned in school with what is experienced in his life. The teacher often sets an example by relating a personal experience, and then gets the children to talk about it: "What would you have done if you had been me?"

A fourth grade art teacher once asked her class to paint a picture of "The Teacher's Treasure." She brought out her old, dirty, and much-used mountaineering boots and put them on her desk. At first the children couldn't believe that these were a "treasure." But the teacher told them stories of her college days when she would go to the mountains to hike, and regaled them with tales of her adventures with wild animals, of camping with friends, of the happiness she felt in the clean mountain air. The children were enraptured, and while their paintings may not have been technically skilled, they had color and feeling: the boots had become real and important to them.

Some teachers are not so successful. Another fourth grade teacher tried to get her class to sing a fall song about red maple leaves. She brought some leaves mounted on a large sheet of white paper and asked her class to "describe how wonderful they are." Dead silence followed, and then a few children, helping her out, tried to respond. Dead leaves, a dead exercise, and instead of motivation, only pity.

FIRE AND AIR: A SCIENCE CLASS

A fifth-grader, of course, has to be motivated differently. Here a teacher may need only to be open to the children's response. As we see fifth grade science students finding their places at the laboratory tables, the teacher, a man in his late forties dressed in a white lab coat, asks for their attention and then puts a question: "What do you think will happen when you put a bottle over a burning candle?" All hands go up, and he calls on five or six children, noting their responses but approving or disapproving none. He writes down all of the speculations on a blackboard, after which he sends the children to get bottles, candles, matches, and some water to extinguish flames. He asks paired sets of children to light the candle, to place the bottle upside-down over it, and to observe what happens. They do, and note that the candle goes out.

Most of the children aren't content with that simple observation and introduce some variations, such as lifting the bottle a little, blowing under it, and so on. Others count the seconds it takes for the flame to die out. The teacher allows them to experiment, but keeps asking "Why did it go out?" The children all want him to visit their tables, to check the experiments they've devised, to answer questions. He answers no questions, except with more questions, or he asks that they try doing the exercise again. He insists that they all listen to each other's observations and queries, and finally asks for several of the teams to present their own trials, and their hypotheses about the results to the class. In turn, each team goes to the front desk, sets up the equipment, and demonstrates what it did—some holding the bottle at different heights, others lowering the bottle suddenly. The teacher now asks what there is about the bottle, its position, the flame, the candle, or anything else affecting the circumstances that makes the flame go out sooner rather than later. Some children raise their hands, he calls on them, and they respond with a variety of answers. He then draws a diagrammatic representation of the experiment on the board. Each team comes forward and provides explanations in firm, complete, and confident phrasing. The teacher also asks questions of those who haven't raised their hands, and some try to respond. But those who have nothing to say are in no way singled out and put on the spot.

The class then takes a ten-minute recess, since this is a double science session of two forty-minute periods. They then return noisily for the second session, which starts with a formal bow to the teacher. The ritual marks a clear break from the noise and a renewal of focus on the task of the day.

The children take up the question again, and this time the teacher asks if they know anything about oxygen, and the relationship between the flame and the air. The children answer somewhat tentatively, even though a few know a lot (most have only a sketchy acquaintance). The teacher surprises a daydreaming child by asking him a question in a rather peremptory tone. The child sits up suddenly, blushes, and has no answer. The teacher has been tough and sudden, and shocks everyone. He quickly resumes the friendly, Socratic tone established earlier.

For the last half-hour of the class, the children are asked to begin a report of the experiment. They take out paper, rulers, pencils, and start to draw the experiment and then to describe and explain it. After giving explicit instructions about how a proper laboratory report is prepared, the teacher moves around the room to advise and correct. The product is a lab report, half-finished today but to be completed at home. The children worked in pairs during most of the class, but the report is an individual assignment.

The teacher here demands a lot of his students but dictates very little. His lesson is the scientific method, and the experiment is a device by which method is taught rather than a conclusive demonstration of oxidation. Though this man is not one of the teachers in the school who "kid around" with the students, he is not known to intimidate. His method is exploration, but the limits are clear: children are not encouraged to go far beyond the constraints the materials themselves provide. And yet, the children are encouraged to push to the margin, to devise all the variations that their imaginations can bring to bear on the materials.

Thus, science in the Japanese elementary school is taught not through rote learning, but through direct experience, observation, and experiment. The curriculum is organized so that children's earliest experiences with science are gained through "friendly," everyday materials. In the first and second grades, children raise plants and observe the weather, and acquaint themselves with such basic principles as magnetism. They work through increasingly complex phenomena, principles, and contexts, so that by the sixth grade they are dealing with the basics of biology, physics, and chemistry.

The Value of Engaged Effort

Japanese elementary school pedagogy, like maternal socialization, is based on the belief that the teacher's job is to get all children to commit themselves wholeheartedly to hard work. In the United States, a teacher is expected to evaluate individual ability and to praise any level of accomplishment, even in the face of mistakes. In Japan, if the child gets 99 out of 100 right, the teacher will still say, "Not perfect, but it could be so if you *really* pay attention."

American educational rhetoric does invoke the idea of "the whole child," value "self-expression," and promote emotional engagement in "discovery learning." But Japanese teaching style, at least in primary schools, employs all three in a mode that surpasses most American efforts. In the cubing class, I was struck by the spontaneity, excitement, and (to American eyes) unruly dedication of the children to the new idea. I was similarly impressed with the teacher's ability to create the mood. What's going on reflects cultural assumptions. American pedagogy usually separates cognition and emotional affect, and then devises artificial means for reintroducing "feeling" into abstract mastery. It is rather like the way canned fruit juices are produced—first denatured by the preserving process and then injected with vitamins to replace what was lost. The way Japanese culture works is more holistic.

As early as 1919, John Dewey also observed the absence of overt discipline in Japanese classrooms:

> They have a great deal of freedom there, and instead of the children imitating and showing no individuality—which seems to be the proper thing to say— I never saw so much variety and so little similarity in drawings and other handwork, to say nothing of its quality being much better than the average of ours. The children were under no visible discipline, but were good as well as happy; they paid no attention to visitors. . . . I expected to see them all rise and bow.[6]

The children in such a class *are* good as well as happy, since no one has taught them that any contradiction exists between the two. But it sometimes seems that American classrooms, and American parents as well, teach a different lesson: that goodness results from inhibition rather than joy, and that the demands on a child to be good cannot be consonant with whatever produces happiness. The kind of good-natured teasing and kidding, the uproarious noise that fills the Japanese classroom, the wrestling and hugging with the teacher after class, are clearly evidence of "happiness," but no one is "out of line." To be "in line" in an American classroom may mean no joy—the only source of which, sometimes, is behavior and forms of expression that are explicitly proscribed.

SOCIAL LESSONS

The Japanese goals of the classroom engagement are early emotional maturity, compliance, and social courtesy, as well as engagement for its own sake. All this implies self-reliance, which seems to us inconsistent with compliant dependency. However, the "self" on which the child must learn to rely is in service to the social environment in which he must fit completely: thus, the child faces no real conflict.

For the Japanese child, social lessons are everywhere to be found, meaning that all activities during the school day are valued, not just those with explicit academic content. From the moment a child arrives until he leaves, every school-day performance and exchange is part of the learning experience. Earthquake drills are a good example.[7] Out of the PA system comes a sudden rumbling noise, the noise of a simulated earthquake. Children reach for their padded hoods, made by their mothers on a pattern provided by the school, or for their hard hats, provided by the school, and huddle under their desks. Later a whistle blows an all-clear signal and the children line up in pairs to file out into the schoolyard. There, after roll call is taken, parents sometimes come to collect smaller children; mothers have been alerted ahead of time, their availability for such events being all but mandatory. In short, the school and family have worked together to ensure the security of the children. In the well-coordinated action taken by all to prepare for the drill, as well as from the drill itself, everyone learns an important lesson: for a vulnerable nation, cooperation is a matter of life or death.

IMAGINE THIS FISH IN THE SEA

The Japanese teacher, like his charges, is given limits to how much he can invent within the curriculum. Yet Japanese teachers push themselves to present the material imaginatively, and most of all, to emphasize common sense and the relevance of whatever is taught to the everyday lives of the students.

A fourth grade social studies teacher, for example, devised a way to study something required on pisciculture and the Japanese fishing industry. He began class by dumping the contents of a shopping bag on the front desk. In the bag were fish of all kinds and supermarket packets of shrimp and other shellfish. The desk was covered with limp and smelly things. The teacher then turned on a projector to show a chart on the wall, which was a diagrammatic representation of the Japanese coastline with indications of sea depth. He pointed out to the children where each of the fish on his desk might have been caught, at what depth they lived, and by what means fish at different depths are caught. He showed them how far fishermen have to go to get different species, and what habits these fish have. As he talked, he constantly invited interruption and excitedly waved the fish in front of children's faces. This, of course, elicited cries of disgust, as some of the girls retreated under their desks.

The teacher was not told by the ministry of education's curriculum guidelines to provide examples of fish "in the flesh." Neither was he told to use the drama produced by a darkened room and projected images, nor to say anything about how fish are caught. By the end of the class, the children could recognize the fish and say something about their lives and habits, as well as the way fishermen go about making a living. And the smell of the fish would remain in the classroom for several hours, which could only remind the children of the lengths to which their teacher would go to help them understand.

This lesson in pisciculture is a good example of what Japanese teachers do to provide *sogo katsudo*, "integrated activities," for their classrooms. Elementary school teachers often put together interdisciplinary assaults on a theme. In the school where the abovementioned lesson took place, the social studies class considers the broad question of the importance of fish to Japanese life, the science class takes up the biology of fish, and the language class is devoted to writing stories about fish. For the third-grader in the same school, the theme is paper making. Children learn how paper is made, make their own, visit a paper factory, and in art class use paper in many ways as a medium. *Sogo katsudo* is an example of the freedom to innovate that can exist within a standardized Japanese curriculum.

HOME AND SCHOOL

In home and school, learning reinforces human relationships and provides other emotional rewards. The lesson of supportive environments is that it is very important and entirely appropriate to be fully engaged in and excited by participation. Though Japanese children are thought to be obsessed by the prospect of exams that loom, in fact one finds little explicit stress on the distant future. Meanwhile, teachers spend time with the family of each of their charges, responsible for knowing the whole context of the child's life. While some teachers complain that mothers pressure children at home to study—"Don't play. Do your homework first!"—they genuinely feel that their own way of getting children involved works for any grade level or level of ability. Teachers suggest to mothers that they let the school handle the child's motivation.

Nevertheless, life at home mostly supports life at school constructively, except when it comes to handling examination anxiety. The examinations often involve parents in a child's education as early as elementary school. Parents can sometimes wield influence to get their offspring into the right middle schools, which are, of course, those with the best record of admission into the best high schools. And these are known by how many of their graduates enter the most prestigious colleges and universities.

But before exam anxieties begin in earnest, the mother as a member of the community comprising the school is very much caught up in her child's learning, and in most cases is as eager as the teacher to make the experience happy and relaxed, to engage rather than force or push the child. In that frame of mind, a mother will help her child with homework after school and in the evenings. This is usually regarded as positively integral to his education. The Japanese child needs maternal guidance and support, and the mother gets much satisfaction from helping him. But some teachers now say that they don't know who's being graded, the mother or the child.

Two Portraits

Two portraits, that of a third grade boy from a traditional shopkeeper's family and that of a sixth grader already on a path to college, show us something about home and school during the elementary school years.

Jiro of the Bean Curd Shop

Jiro is an eight-year-old third grader living in Osaka. He is the second son of a bean curd maker and his wife, who run a small shop in an older quarter of the city. Jiro's mother's father, a semi-invalid, lives with the family in their apartment behind the shop. The business consists of a front room facing the street—a room with cedar vats for soaking the soybeans, a motor-driven grinder, cauldrons to boil the beans, presses for making the tofu, and a small counter where customers are served. In a back room are sacks of beans and other supplies. The establishment is well known locally for its traditional bean curd; and even some suburban Osakans occasionally come here to buy. The shop has been in Jiro's family for four generations, ever since his great-great grandfather was adopted into the family as heir.

Jiro and his elder brother and younger sister have been raised among the sacks and in the steamy smells of tofu production. The older boy, now eleven years, will take over the shop upon his father's retirement and already works with him after school, waiting on customers during the late afternoon "housewives' rush hour." His mother keeps the books, cleans the shop morning and evening, takes care of her father's needs, and chats with customers. The tofu making itself is Jiro's father's job, at least to supervise, but the moment of curd formation is considered a sacred time which mobilizes the whole household.

Jiro's job is to do well in school, because his future depends on his wits, not on inheritance. His parents hope he'll get a job in a large company and become an admired "salaryman." But they train him at home in the skills of a shopkeeper, just in case, and because shopkeeping is what they know. Jiro is very much encouraged to develop the skills of human relationships, for it is by maintaining warm ties with customers and neighbors that his parents feel the shop prospers. He is taught, at least by example, to remember everyone's name and their regular order; he also observes how his mother prepares gifts for people who have just moved into the neighborhood, as well as ceremonial gifts for old customers at holiday times. She always has hot water for tea ready whenever someone stops in. At slow times, she will make the rounds of the other neighborhood shops of various kinds, to cement relationships with the owners. In times of crisis, she must count on them.

Jiro also learns from his mother how to keep the books. She herself learned on the *soroban* (abacus), but recently the family has purchased a small personal computer. Jiro loves to use it, but his mother discourages him, saying that he must learn to do the accounting in the old way, or at least with paper and pencil.

Jiro's school is nearby, and he walks there every day with his brother. Jiro is in Mrs. Okayama's third grade. His favorite subject is art, and he sketches nearly all day in the margins of his workbooks and on scraps of paper. In art class he is consistently commended for his work, but is also consistently reminded that he has a lot to learn. He is often chided for scribbling in his books. When the teacher assigned a project to the class in two-person teams, he and his friend composed and crafted a book of poems and sketches. The teacher was amazed at their skills and had the boys present it to the school. When Jiro and his friend took the project to the principal's office for the presentation, Jiro was nervous but proud. No one before in the class had ever been honored in this way. Jiro's mother and father were proud too, but quietly hoped the school would not encourage Jiro to become an artist: too risky a future.

Mrs. Okayama devotes the most class time to Japanese language, averaging one hour or more per day. The children are learning characters, and by the end of the third grade they will know about four hundred. But this is still not enough to read a newspaper, which requires about nineteen hundred. The books they read use characters plus *furigana,* or syllabic transliterations for characters they don't yet know.

Next to Japanese, the subject most emphasized is arithmetic, with four sessions per week and regular homework. Science and social studies follow, then music and art. (Physical education is given as much time as science and social studies.) The social studies curriculum covers a wide range of topics in an exploratory, interdisciplinary way. Children in the first grade usually start with an investigation of the local neighborhood and work out to their city, their prefecture, and their region. As the pupils grow older, social studies encompasses even larger geographical units, and moves back in time as well.

Neither Jiro nor his brother attend *juku.* They both get good grades in school, and for now their parents are satisfied, but there is talk of sending Jiro's brother to *juku* when he gets to junior high school. For even if he will eventually inherit the shop, the parents hope he can go to a good high school, which confers prestige on the family. It is Jiro whom they hope to send to college, so that he can enter a company, and he, too, will start *juku* in junior high school. His days, for now, are pleasant and unpressured, and he and his friends play after school before doing the evening's homework.

Tomoko at the Brink

Now let's look at a sixth grade girl, nearing the end of her elementary school career, as she looks forward to entering middle school.

Five and a half years have passed since she was a timid first-grader, awed and excited by a new world. She is now a confident and accomplished student, seeing the school as a "family" that she is rather hesitant to leave.

To begin the second term of the sixth grade, Tomoko has returned to school after summer vacation. During that time, she, like nearly all her classmates, worked hard to maintain and advance her skills by taking classes in tutoring school and by reading and studying at home. Her class, along with all her teachers, also took a trip together to a hot-spring resort near the sea, and this was the high point of her summer. Her family took a one-week vacation to visit her uncle and his family on his tangerine farm in Shizuoka prefecture. Upon returning to school, she brought her summer notebooks, her summer science project (an insect collection), and an essay she wrote about the class trip.

Tomoko has been with her group of classmates for five and a half years—indeed with some since kindergarten. She knows them well, and although her friendships wax and wane in intensity and she seems to have a different "best friend" every year, they are still all her friends, and that sense of family was further enhanced during the class summer excursion.

Tomoko lives with her family, including her younger brother (a second-grader at the same school), in a condominium near the school. Her father, an executive in a general trading company, has spent much of the past eighteen months overseas, first in Oslo and then in Saudi Arabia. He was earlier asked by his company to help set up an office in Europe for two years, but he and his wife felt that the risks of taking their children out of Japanese schools outweighed the potential benefits (extra pay, for one). He declined (with some risk of losing promotional ground) and accepted instead a somewhat less prestigious "roving" position, which would allow him to return to Japan frequently. He says that if an overseas posting had been proposed when the children were very small he might have taken it, for he hopes that they can be more "international" in outlook. At this stage, however, he feels that Tomoko, especially, ought to stay in a Japanese school to ensure that she will be able to go to a good high school and university. Although he does not want to intensify prematurely the anxiety of the examinations to come, he feels that a long-range perspective on the children's future, which accounts for pressures on the horizon, is necessary. So, for the time being, Tomoko's mother is in sole charge of the household, and although the grandmother lives nearby and can help out occasionally, the children's educational lives are the mother's responsibility. Tomoko hopes that her father will be home for her sixth grade graduation in March.

The second term begins in the first week of September. The first day starts with a school assembly in the schoolyard, less formal than the opening of the year in April, but with a special message to sixth-graders from the principal. He reminds them that because this is their last term in the school, they must apply themselves to their work and to their friendships to make the year a meaningful and productive one.

Early in the morning, Tomoko and her friends choose to meet at a corner a few blocks from school, to enjoy a walk together. The younger children also meet at set locations in each neighborhood for the same purpose. Even getting to school is hence a lesson in community. Not to join *some* group on the way to school is a bit antisocial, or means that one arrives too early or too late, neither of which is good.

Tomoko's schedule is a busy one. She has classes in Japanese language (five classroom sessions per week), in social studies (three per week), in math, science, domestic science, sports, and music. She also works on the yearbook committee, and will have to help to prepare the copy for the book in only a few weeks. She has been chosen *toban* for about a month and feels both proud and nervous about the responsibility.

The *toban* is the leader of the class. The method of selection and the length of the term vary greatly from school to school. The children chosen to be *toban* and other class officers are often given preferment by virtue of their academic ranking, meaning that social responsibility and personal success are strongly connected. In some schools, the term is short and many children are given an opportunity to serve. Tomoko must meet with the teacher regularly to talk about matters that come up in class discussions, and issues perceived to be problems by students and the teacher. The *toban* also helps organize class outings, skits, and other events.

Last term there was a significant problem in a class that the *toban* had to help monitor. One boy had teased another child, whose mother is Korean, and the hazing had taken on a racial cast. The teacher had overheard remarks at recess in the schoolyard, and had brought the two children together to talk about it. It turned out, according to the weeping victim, that this was not the first time a child had "called him names"; accordingly, the teacher decided that a class discussion was needed.

Since there was then (and is now) in the press much coverage of *ijime,* or "bullying," the parents and teachers of the school were especially on the alert to any incident that might fall in the category. Their school had been free of such incidents up to then, and they wanted to nip this one in the bud.

There was an open-ended discussion in class, during which children presented their views of the situation and a heated debate developed about when children should solve their own problems and when they should be brought to adult attention. Some resolution was achieved. The children were asked to imagine how the victim felt, and to put themselves in his place, feeling his pain and his anger. They were asked to judge whether there had been any provocation, and whether the children who were teasing had any other reason to be acting out their feelings in this way. Only once were the perpetrators singled out, and they expressed sorrow at having teased the victim. Finally, the teacher asked the class to remember the importance of the sixth grade in the school; younger children look up to them for guidance and for examples of good behavior. The teacher and students together expressed a hope that such episodes would not blemish their own and the school's record again. Tomoko hopes that she will not have to help adjudicate such a crisis in her term as *toban.*

Tomoko's daily job at the start of the term is to help sweep the halls of the sixth grade's corridor. Children are responsible for cleaning the school. Not having maintenance crews, Japanese schools rely on the children to tend the rooms and halls; outside tradesmen arrive only for major cleaning and repairs. At some schools, the work is done in the early morning; at others, during the last period of the day. Children wear smocks and dust scarves over their hair; they sweep, dust the desks and other surfaces, and wet-mop the floors of halls and classrooms.

Children also serve lunch. Most schools do not have cafeterias, since space is at a premium, and lunch is eaten in the classroom. The hot lunch is picked up by a team of children, while the rest arrange the desks to form group "tables." The servers wear white smocks and usually caps and face masks. Lunch is usually not what we would consider "traditional Japanese" fare, but is usually bread, a main dish with some sort of meat, and a vegetable, along with milk. A typical meal at Tomoko's school: bread, margarine and marma-lade; chop suey with pork and vegetables; a boiled egg and milk. Rice is almost never served, to the consternation of domestic rice growers; but since most of Japan's rice is now imported, it is no longer a local industry. Another group of chores gives children a sense of the importance of nature in their lives: children are responsible for caring for the school's animals and the garden that they have planted. Usually these tasks are taken care of in the early morning.

At recess, which is really an exercise break, children go out in all kinds of weather to perform calisthenics, led by teachers. Many teachers regularly wear exercise clothes and warm-up suits to school, so it is hard to tell who is the physical education teacher and who the science teacher.

Outside of school, Tomoko has several activities. Classes finish at 2:30, and on some days Tomoko stays later for extracurricular pursuits. On others she arrives home at 2:45, on Tuesdays and Thurs-days leaving after a snack for her *juku* class—afternoon sessions at a small neighborhood tutoring school where she does extra work in math and has also begun to study English, a subject that she will formally begin in middle school next year. She is interested in having a job which will allow her to travel, and daydreams about being a stewardess or tour guide, or in grander reveries, about working for the United Nations.

Tomoko's *juku* class meets from 3:30 to 5:00, once a week in math and once in English. The tutoring school is not high-pressured like those attended by some of her classmates, especially the boys, but is aimed at "enhancing" the work she does in school. The English class, she says, is fun, and she enjoys using the language tapes. This year's "best friend" is taking the English class with her, and they take the bus home together, practicing their English noisily and falling into giggles as they imitate the accent of their instructor.

After the Saturday morning session at regular school, the weekend begins for Tomoko. She has gymnastics lessons during the afternoon, at a special gymnasium on the other side of the city, founded by a former Olympic gymnast, a Mrs. Ikeda. This class is very demanding, and the teachers have high expectations for the girls. Tomoko feels very anxious as the time for the spring gymnastics meet approaches, and she often cannot eat or sleep just before it. She once broke a toe in an event, but the tension before and embarrassment after the accident far exceeded the physical pain. The tone and feeling of the school is very similar to that of the fast-track *juku* that prepare children for the exams to the best high schools and universities, and the message is the same: doing your best is not enough, but with effort and the right attitude, one can exceed all standards.

Although Tomoko's evenings are spent studying, she watches an hour or so of television—usually one of the pop song shows featuring stars who are not much older than she. Her Sunday recreation time may be spent with her family, because it is her father's day off too, or she may go shopping with her friends, looking for records, clothes, and the latest "paraphernalia" for schoolgirls presented by the large department stores in a special section—keychains, school bag "mascots," handkerchiefs, decorated pencil cases, anything at all with a Snoopy motif or the latest cartoon character.[8]

Tomoko is not especially interested in boys. While her American counterparts might be dressing up, trying on some makeup, even in extreme cases participating in sexual encounters, Tomoko and her friends see boys as classmates, sometimes as pals, and sometimes as nuisances. In American terms we might say that Japanese children have a delayed adolescence, or—possibly—none at all. High schoolers, as Thomas Rohlen points out, are called "children" (*kodomo*), and although there are words in Japanese for "youths," people in their teens, if they are still in school, are not "dignified" by such a term, nor set apart as "teenagers."[9]

Tomoko's last term in elementary school will most likely be a positive and happy experience, full of real cheer. She is headed for a nearby middle school, not an elite or prestigious one, but one where her parents feel she will receive what she needs to get into a good high school, since she herself seems highly motivated in her studies. Tomoko has never discussed where she will go beyond middle school but assumes she'll attend a good high school and college.

Tomoko's parents have not pushed her. Her attendance at the *juku*, at least in the math class, was generated not out of anxiety that she might fall behind, but because her teacher at school said she might be understimulated in the sixth grade curriculum. Anyway, her friends were all taking extra classes. There are examples in her class at school of children who *are* experiencing more school-related tension. Tetsuo, a boy who has strong interests in science, takes *juku* classes every afternoon, for his parents expect that he may have a chance at entering a national university, and think perhaps Tsukuba, a science-oriented university, would be appropriate. Tetsuo will attempt to enter a middle school out of the neighborhood, whose entrance rate into the best local high school is known to be high. It is fair to say that parents tend to focus more on boys' "talents" in school and to attempt to provide them with the best environment. While the educational future of girls is of course attended to, and admission into a good school is of great importance, the ladders are different, and ultimately, the investment in first-rate education not seen as important for girls.

Secondary school represents a major departure from the modes and content of learning experienced in elementary school. Tomoko and her friends are aware that they are about to leave a place and period in their lives where harmony and warmth are of primary significance and where cooperation is more highly valued than competition. The next three years in middle school, and the following three in high school, loom as periods of serious effort and testing, characterized at best as challenging, and at worst as a devastatingly harsh environment in which one's future becomes mapped.

8

SECONDARY SCHOOLS

A Crisis of Engagement

Dear Beth:

I'm almost 13. Dad won't allow me to do anything, even listen to rock music or watch TV. . . . My school grades aren't terrible—C's and D's—but because of them I lose all privileges, even sleeping over at my friends'. Sometimes I think about killing him!

—Angry

Dear Angry:

That's a lousy solution. A more mature reaction is to consider whether you'd win more freedom by getting better marks. Going to school is a serious job for kids. Your dad should not ignore your mediocre performance. Show him you are growing up by putting more energy into school work, instead of into revenge, and your life could improve both at home and at school.[1]

How can we interpret the above "dialogue" as a cultural artifact of our secondary school environment? And how might the exchange be seen through Japanese eyes? What is the meaning of secondary schooling for a typical American child and his parents? Here I want to talk about the environment and cultural context of schooling in Japanese secondary schools, and, by comparing American and Japanese expectations and experiences, attempt to explain why the content of the advice column would seem so alien in Japan.

The thirteen-year-old who wrote the letter is presumably "under-performing," not realizing her potential, as her teachers would say. Her father has laid down the law and set up conditions for her life outside of school, focused, we assume, on an improvement in her grades. Her desires seem harmless and predictable enough: sitcoms on TV, standard pop music, and time with her friends. She is presumably not a juvenile delinquent, simply an unmotivated underachiever. She might represent a significant percentage of the middle-school population in America.

Her reaction to her father's curtailment of her activities is also predictable: she is furious. Because she begins by saying how old she is, she apparently thinks that she is too old to be treated this way, that she shouldn't be punished, and that she should be allowed to run her own life. She feels, it would seem, entitled to make her own choices, and is indignant at the way her father has tried to make her a child. She must expect sympathy from newspaper readers, for she has written to an advice columnist who publishes letters. And this is clear evidence that she and her father fundamentally disagree what a girl her age should be doing with her life. It is also clear that she simply has no idea what might be valued aside from what she wants. In her eyes, her father is an old fogey and a tyrant, so he could not be acting out of any real concern for her welfare or education.

"Beth's" response is interesting too. At first glance, we might suppose that Japanese parents would agree with her, taking the part of the father. But it is clear that Beth feels the only way to reach the letter writer is to appeal to her desire for freedom and pleasure. The headline for the column reads: "Harder work, better grades could bring more privileges." And therein lies one source of incentive and motivation for the American student—to use real and potential achievement as a bargaining chip with parents. The Japanese parent would agree that "going to school is a serious job for kids" and would expect a child to take responsibility for schoolwork as a sign of maturity, just as do "Beth" and the father in the scenario. But in Japan, very few lines are drawn between parent and child; moreover, school is very seldom an arena into which family battles are extended. And finally, good grades are virtually never used as currency to buy perks.

So what does happen in Japanese secondary school? For one thing, most children do not in any way see their parents and teachers as antagonists and school as any kind of battleground. Moreover, in attitude polls conducted among children of several countries, Japanese children scored highest in "liking school." Most children seem to feel that school is a good place to be and that the activities which go on there are appropriate. They also genuinely want to improve their own educational performance. There are, of course, children who do not want to go to school; cases of children who have developed "school phobia" are played up in the Japanese media. This is odd. In the United States, school dropouts and other school-related pathologies are matters of some concern to editorial writers, but not much. Statistically, we have a problem to which we don't devote attention; the Japanese don't have such a problem but the matter is nevertheless sensationalized.

Japanese Problems and Their Treatment

But some Japanese problems, in some ways at least, parallel those of the American thirteen-year-old. "School refusal syndrome" is much discussed in Japan. The term encompasses a wide range of behavior in which children resist going to school. They sometimes exhibit physical symptoms (most frequently, stomachaches) and are permitted to stay home; at other times they are simply truant without permission. Margaret Lock notes that the rate of long-term absence from junior high in 1982 was only 0.36 percent of all students.[2] Nevertheless, professional counselors, educators, and psychotherapists usually view the school refusal syndrome as a psychiatric expression of deviance, and the therapeutic goal is, of course, to get the child back into school. Dr. Lock's study shows that most Japanese believe the problem stems from the intensity of the nuclear family—particularly from overindulgent mothers devoted, to the exclusion of all else, to their children. In any case, Lock says that children who are low achievers or underachievers are especially vulnerable. Some Japanese experts say the cause is diet: the "junk food" that is more and more ingested by children is said to produce lethargy and "nervous exhaustion" in children already highly stressed.

In the United States, heavy consumption of junk food is said to produce hyperactivity in children. The fact is that the actual content of junk food does differ to some small degree in the United States and Japan. But if it is consumed, the Japanese fear disengagement and apathy; we fear uncontrollable, wild behavior. For the record, the ministry of education asserts that the home environment and the absent father are the key factors making for school refusal.

Other perceived problems in Japan include dramatic violence that may be directed against teachers (or against parents at home). A child in middle school (most frequently in the third year of middle school) will attack a teacher physically and occasionally kill him. The statistical incidence is very small, but again highly publicized. One recently discussed case was that of a boy who had been at school overseas with his parents. He was sent back to Japan to live with his uncle and aunt, to attend a Japanese middle school. The pressure on him to conform to Japanese practices and expectations after a sojourn abroad was said to have been too great, and he killed the uncle and aunt. These cases are seen on the whole to be the product of individual pathologies, but are still the subject of much public soul searching.

Suicide among children is the most sensational phenomenon attributed in the Japanese press to educational pressures. Until recently, juvenile suicide was most commonly linked to personal failure in the examinations, especially among college aspirants. But the rate has declined among the fifteen- to twenty-year-old age group, leaving causality mongers among the Japanese somewhat confused. Since 1980 the United States has led Japan in juvenile suicides for fifteen- to twenty-year-olds, at 12.5 per 100,000 to Japan's 10.8 per 100,000. In fact, there is no consistent relationship between the Japanese deaths and *shiken jigoku,* or "examination hell."

Americans, of course, are unlikely to consider school pressure important in a high schooler's suicide, and usually stress psychological and family factors. In contrast, the Japanese easily regard the examination as *the* precipitating factor, given other personal pathologies or family crises. In recent years, however, a new etiology for juvenile suicides has emerged, and this is the increase of peer pressure in schools. This recently publicized phenomenon, called *ijime,* or "bullying," has come to receive almost daily headlines in Japan: children, primarily in middle school, teasing and beating each other. The problem is not new anywhere in the world. British public schools are, of course, notorious for the hazing of new entrants, who must "take it like a man" as a way to membership in the group. Traditionally in Japan, too, high schools such as the famous Ichiko in Tokyo tolerated or even encouraged elaborate ceremonies of bullying.[3]

The case today appears different, however; less ritualized and definitely no part of a *rite de passage*. Japanese analysts attribute the presumed crisis of *ijime* first to personality problems among the victimized, then to pressures in school, and finally to insufficient succor and support from adults in the bullied child's life at home and at school. There is in all of this a certain amount of blaming the victim. In fact, Japanese psychologists assert that children who are hounded by others, sometimes to death, are different in that they have "dark personalities": secretive and quiet, they do not make good members of a group.

Recent examples include that of a thirteen-year-old middle school girl who hung herself from a cord attached to a utility pole. What was responsible? Having ostracized the girl, her classmates continued to taunt her by writing epithets in her textbooks. They even threw stones at her house. The tormentors were her "friends," girls in her class. Another victim, a sixteen-year-old high school boy in Osaka, was beaten and drowned in a river. He had been killed with a hammer by two classmates whom he had teased and tormented by painting their faces and whipping them with a belt. The two cases of *ijime* are extreme and obviously make good press, but milder cases are an everyday matter in some schools.

Teachers and parents have been slow to notice incidents of *ijime*, and the reported numbers are indeed slight: out of 15,000 middle and high schools, only 531 cases were reported in 1984—hardly the stuff of American "blackboard jungles." However, a survey of Japanese and American junior high schools showed that 58 percent of the American students had been teased, ostracized, or assaulted by classmates, compared to 40 percent of the Japanese.[4] Among the latter Japanese cases, seven children committed suicide, and these suicides were attributed to verbal and psychological abuse by other children. Eighty percent of the *ijime* incidents occurred among junior high school students. Of the total, one-third were perpetrated by girls. Most of the cases involved the use of force, including 196 cases of injury: 112 of violence by individuals and 81 by groups. Ninety-nine involved threats and blackmail. One important difference between the two countries is that in America other students and teachers tend to intervene if possible; in Japan other students rarely become involved and simply observe. Japanese teachers are also afraid that if they step in, they may themselves be attacked. For Japanese psychologists, *ijime* demonstrates that the existing system of education does not harness energies and ambitions appropriately.

Similarly, an editorial in the *Asahi Shimbun*, a leading national paper, suggests that the children who bully are tormenting "weaker" children who are in some way "different"—and the system is responsible. Japanese children are being taught, the newspaper continues, that uniformity is necessary and prized, that deviance is to be eradicated; and so, under pressure to homogenize themselves, Japanese schoolchildren try to homogenize others. Putting it another way, the *Far Eastern Economic Review* says: "If such pressure to conform is internalized unwillingly, it is bound to want release. And what could be a handier vent than a friend or acquaintance who seems to be out of step with the group and in need of discipline?"[5]

In general, however, public discussion centers on the victim. And great efforts are made to analyze the *higaisha ishiki,* or "victim mentality." This mentality is possessed, the thinking goes, by weaker, non-conformist, or slower students, who "provoke" attacks because of their marginality. There is less concern about the personality and motivation of the perpetrators, whose acts are seen simply as a violent expression of the majority's reaction to "differentness."

The anxiety about the problem is so widespread that the evening television news regularly reports current incidents and statistics by type of abuse, gender of participants, location, and actions taken. All this is accompanied by graphs and charts that resemble those used in weather forecasts. Thus alarmed, sixty percent of parents in Maebashi City took out a new kind of *ijime* insurance coverage for their children, which was later canceled by city councilmen, who claimed that the policies protect the bullies. Finally, the intense media interest and concern has led the ministry of education to create a committee on *ijime* that will conduct extensive research on the problem.

If the victimizer seldom receives Japanese commentary, neither do school conditions or other broad social contexts. Suggested therapy or solutions to *ijime* come down on factors that would seem easy to correct and avoid any that might address structural change in the society at large. Thus a mother is blamed for her "selfishness"—too much anxious attention paid to her own child's success—but the psychosocial problem of her isolation in a small apartment in a large, anonymous housing complex is largely ignored.

Of course, the general problem of examination hell and *ijime* is discussed: a set of forbidding exams stands between junior high and high school, and another between high school and college. But *ijime* occurs more often in junior high school than in high school, where the exam anxiety runs higher. So something else is also at work here. In any case, Japanese commentators do see examination hell as a significant source of emotional strain, but their commentary remains curiously abstract. Why is that? Because any discussion of the exams leads to a paralyzing sense of helplessness in face of the educational-occupational system that depends on testing as a means of selection. In general, given problems some Japanese children and their parents experience in school and at home, the preferred response stresses personal, not social, deficiencies.

COMPARISONS

The American child who wrote the "Dear Beth" letter and the Japanese child who committed suicide are both adolescents, both students in schools that try to help students realize potential in life. Are both school systems so at odds with adult goals, creating such tension, that motivation, energy, and even lives are at risk? Do American and Japanese problems differ?

Americans tend to believe that Japanese children, driven by the specter of the exams, are hounded by teachers and parents into nonstop studying; so compulsive are the young Japanese overachievers that no time is left for play or even for sleep. Automata, they work so hard that life becomes only a set of multiple choice questions to be answered at exam time. We further assume that Japanese children are permanently damaged by the pressure: suicidal at worst, obsessive at best.

Another view espoused by some Japanese and Westerners has it that if we compare the Japanese teenager studying for the exams with an American counterpart, shooting drugs or pregnant out of wedlock and doomed, the effort and commitment of the Japanese child appears in a different light. We need to consider both perspectives, and to weigh the costs and benefits of our cultural assumptions and our educational institutions by experiencing them as the child does. Since most of us think that exams color all aspects of Japanese education, we need to talk about their place in secondary school experience.

THE EXAMINATIONS

The testing that marks the transition from middle to high school and from high school to college is both a legacy from an ancient feudal society committed to education and a product of modern egalitarianism. The Chinese examination system, from which the Japanese system is derived, acted as a selector of elite talent for the imperial administrative bureaucracy.[6] The Chinese-derived exams were not open to all, but the cohorts of permitted aspirants were assured of a meritocratic appraisal of their efforts.

In the Meiji period, the Japanese opened access to the exams to anyone who could pass threshold levels of competency. The justification for the reform in a precedent-conscious society was that the country needed its best and brightest, a trained and talented elite to bring Japan into a competitive or at least dignified place in the industrializing world. Japan's natural resources were scarce and her "island mentality"—a sense of both vulnerability and uniqueness—produced a unified and concerted drive to catch up with the modern world.

For three hundred years before the Meiji Restoration in 1868, Japan had been a closed feudal, and relatively decentralized country, but mounting internal and external pressure after 1853 created a panicky energy and readiness for change. The vehicle for that change became the *human* resource developed through education: an elite trained in Western sciences and technological skills through a system of qualifications and credentials. Ronald Dore[7] sees the importance of such a program for modernization in a "late-developing" country. Education was already significant in the lives of most of the population. And since the merit principle was relatively unsullied by nepotism or graft, the schools convinced many people to think about self-improvement and to be reasonably optimistic rather than cynical about their chances.

Since the modern Japanese high school is not a part of the compulsory education system, young people take exams to enter even the public high schools. Of course, there are "better" and "worse" high schools and one is placed by tested ability; thus the pressure to acquire exam-appropriate skills. And, although approximately 94 percent of young people attend some kind of high school, the question of one's future is broached as early as the second year of junior high school; for some, earlier. For Japanese twelve-year-olds, a rather abrupt shift occurs from the nurturant, accepting, nondifferentiating style of their early education to the more effort-oriented struggle of secondary schools. In junior high school, children proudly wear uniforms which symbolize the new seriousness of school, but the transition is tough for some. The abruptness may account for the relatively high rate of delinquency and other school-related sociopsychological problems that arise in the third year of middle school.

However, we are wrong to imagine that all Japanese children undergo the worst of the examination hell to which both their media and ours give much column space. In fact, it is estimated that only 10 percent of the relevant Japanese age groups (middle and high school) finds itself in the most heated form of the struggle to get into the top universities. But we shouldn't assume that the rest are taking it easy. To some degree, everyone is committed to his education and his performance in school. What differs is the level and quality of aspiration to which the effort is directed.

The 10 percent who are on the track to the most elite schools are not the tanned and confident "big men on campus" or the children of the landed gentry. They are those who are either superbright and in some way most assuredly preparing for university life or those who are bucking the odds, bucking even their own levels of competence to aspire "beyond their best." This latter group of students catches the imagination of the press and public, and to the outside world they look like the obsessive future workaholics who have fired Japanese economic successes. Their energy and do-or-die drive seem inhuman to the rest of us, unwilling perhaps to sacrifice ourselves on the altar of a challenge. It is this group to which the phrase "Pass with four, fail with five" has meaning.

Moreover, it is the overstimulated (by parents or others) and the undersupported (by parents and teachers) within the group of ardent achievers who are vulnerable to the worst psychological effects of the struggle—and who may, in small numbers, become statistics in the suicide rates. In any case, the media, parents, schools, and psychologists, and sometimes the children themselves, attribute juvenile suicides most frequently to the pressure of the examinations.

The examinations are given every March, at which time there is a spate of information, folklore, and gossipy data in the press about the students, their lives and chances. The whole country seems to be watching, coaching, and waiting for the results. The press features photographs of mothers waiting outside examination sites, and stories of crises and tragedies. In 1984 a sixth grader taking an entrance examination into Nada, one of the country's most prestigious secondary schools, experienced a "nervous breakdown" during the exam and had to be taken out by ambulance—a failure at the age of twelve. It turned out that he had been very well prepared indeed, but that his state of anxiety was such that seeing the actual exam triggered total loss of control. There are other such stories, some of children soiling their pants, some of parents themselves breaking down outside the exam building or attacking the examiners and proctors.

One famous story of the recent past was that of a father who took the entrance exams to a university for his daughter, in disguise. He donned a wig and dress, and wore a lot of makeup. Examiners were suspicious but didn't know what to do. After the exam, in which he did very well, he was confronted, since the stubble on his chin showed through the pancake, and he confessed. One not so obvious lesson of the story is that a parent occasionally *is* as committed to a *daughter's* education as to a son's.

Many parents, whether their children are in the fully aspiring 10 percent or not, want to give their children an edge by sending them to *juku*. This has created an inflation in the level of preparation for the exams. Enough children now receive *juku* preparation (86 percent over elementary school age and over 90 percent at high school age in the urban areas) that entrance to the top universities practically *requires* this time-consuming, costly extra training.[8] The attempt to get the edge has also created a phenomenon in which parents attempt to enter their children in prestigious nursery schools so that the children will have a good chance at the best schools all the way up. Dore reports that some of the elite nursery schools now require parents to undergo an entrance examination, since two-year-old children are seen as too young to be tested.[9] The downward extension of the exam pressure has of course created strain on parents and children alike, especially in those families for whom social mobility or maintenance of social status via education is important. Only among the upper-middle-class and very rich parents of Manhattan does a comparable situation exist in the United States.

In fairness to Japanese parents, I should say that nearly all deplore the system and its pressures, but nearly all also feel that they have little choice but to undergo its rigors. The alternative is to refuse to subject their child to the pressure, to opt out of the system, and in so doing severely limit his chances for academic and career success.

The system is said to be out of control, and the times are called the *ranjuku jidai,* or period of "runaway *juku.*" And although recognition of the problem is widespread, it is very difficult to change the system. In fact, parents themselves most often stoutly resist reform; they intensely dislike the current arrangement of things, but they are very much afraid that any radical changes would make their own child's chances even more uncertain.

Finally, as Dore says, with tongue slightly in cheek, the national Japanese leadership may not be really pushing seriously for anything different:

> One suspects that Japan's more conservative leaders, though they are prepared to shake their heads over the system with those who deplore it, are secretly well-satisfied. The examination hell sorts the sheep from the goats; a man who can't take the psychological strain would be no use anyway. . . . And as long as you can keep adolescents in those crucial years when they might otherwise be learning to enjoy themselves, glued to their textbooks from seven in the morning to eleven at night, the society should manage to stave off for quite a long while yet that hedonism which, as everybody knows, destroyed the Roman empire, knocked the stuffing out of Britain, and is currently spreading v.d. through the body politic of the U.S. . . . At least one rather suspects that must be what they are thinking.[10]

Working with the Exam Taker

Mothers, having decided not to buck the system, must somehow encourage their children to study hard every single day after school. A mother assumes some of the psychological burden that must be borne. So she carefully gets her child "on the same side of the fence"; not wanting to become perceived by her child as part of the problem, she makes an alliance with him (joined, ideally, by the child's teachers) against the examination system. Together, as a team, they set out to work as hard as possible to defeat the examinations. The teacher and the mother consult with each other about what methods work best for the child, and the child begins to feel that members of his "team" are in no way trying to pressure him, but are in fact very much on his side against the system. The child, in other words, internalizes the goal of doing well on the exams and works hard not only to please his mother and teacher, but to please himself.

If the child does not do well, he is spared the feeling that the failure was his fault, that he is somehow inferior to those who did do well. Why is he spared a sense of personal inadequacy? Because the Japanese believe that examinations measure only "abilities," which are regarded as separate from the child's "real" self. And so, despite falling short of the mark, the child's identity and feeling of self-worth normally remain unscathed. Moreover, the support and active assistance of the mother and teacher help deflect responsibility from the child; they all suffer, one might say, a "team defeat." Failure is most keenly felt by the mother, who takes the blame upon herself and will often sequester herself at home for weeks, ashamed to go out.

The mother works hard with the child at home to avoid failure: the child is expected to do several hours of homework a night beginning in the upper elementary grades, and this expands to five or six hours a night by high school. The mother is expected to give the child extensive support, and, like the Japanese mothers of Riverdale, New York, studies the same material as the child studies, quizzing him on his lessons, especially during elementary and middle school years. She often brings snacks to her studious youngster, and she may just sit by him, sewing or reading, to keep him company as he works.

A best-selling home study desk for children nicely symbolizes the mother's intense care and the nurturant and protected atmosphere that she, as well as the culture in general, provides learning in Japan. The desk's work space is surrounded on three sides, shielding the child from distraction. There are shelves, and at the front is a dashboard-like arrangement of lights, an electric pencil sharpener, a built-in calculator, and small drawers for equipment. At the far right of the work space is a button connected to a bell mounted in the kitchen for the child to summon his mother for help or a snack.

THE CLASSROOM AND THE *JUKU*

Home tutors (*katei kyoshi*) are also employed if a child is having trouble in a subject. In addition, there are two basic types of extra schooling (*juku*): private remedial classes (*gakushu juku*), for those who have fallen behind, and the better-known examination cram classes (*shingaku juku*), for those who can work at or ahead of the classroom pace and who want to get into a good university. In the latter, the child learns more advanced material to gain an exam advantage over children who study only the regular curriculum.

As we know, unlike the demanding emphasis on developing individual academic abilities in *juku,* the criteria for membership in the regular classroom group are explicitly and defiantly egalitarian. The child is accepted for the person that he is, regardless of the level of his academic abilities. No Japanese child is failed or skipped ahead, and he can be sure of an unquestioned place in his "primary" group of classmates, who stay together as a cohort at least through middle school. So the educational system has produced a split between the "soft" environment of the public school classroom, where noncritical support and harmony reign, and *juku,* where the children are drilled intensively to prepare them for the examinations.

Even the *juku* and *yobiko* (cram schools for children taking a year or more off before the next level of schooling), however, regard emotional engagement as key if a child is to learn. As one researcher in Tokyo put it, the *juku,* if it is a good one, "captures the child's imagination" by using exhortatory language, creating a "campaign atmosphere," asking children to wear sweatbands covered with exertion-inspiring slogans, and sustaining an energetic pace in classroom activity. Hence, the researcher said, the ordinary school is "dull" for the bright student. Good *juku* also exude feelings of cheer, and a fast-track *yobiko,* such as Yoyogi Zemi, aimed at getting its clients into the most prestigious universities, plays Scott Joplin rags in the halls between classes. The point is that pressure and the intensity of competitive endeavor need not always produce fear, anxiety, and alienation, which is something that members of an average American football team at an average American high school know very well.

In any case, the ordinary Japanese classroom teacher has lost an important function, thanks to the separation of school and *juku.* Until recently the teacher was a vital link between school and family, keeping parents abreast of their children's progress and advising them about prospects of getting into a school in the future. In general, the classroom teacher was a moral and social advisor. Now the *juku* teacher, knowing the child less well, and having no overall perspective on his personal background, is in charge of the student's academic (exam-related) progress. This means that the regular teacher, who knows nothing of the child's performance at the *juku,* is often at a loss to help the parents. Some *juku* teachers, however, do take a deep interest in their students.

A Juku *Teacher*

Tadano Sagara has been a *juku* teacher for seventeen years in Toshima-ku, Tokyo. He has a small establishment—a second-floor classroom in his house—that can take eight to ten children. Sagara, age forty-one, is a graduate of Tokyo University's Department of Philosophy. He was a student there during the heat of the student movement of the late 1960s, and when the university closed down for a time he and three friends began a *juku* to earn money until things cooled down. He has been a *juku* teacher ever since. As he himself somewhat ruefully remarks, this is not how a typical Tokyo University graduate makes a living.

Sagara's home sits at the end of a narrow alley. One reaches the classroom by climbing a steep staircase, after leaving one's shoes. The room, full of books and equipment, is tidy but a little shabby, and has small desks and chairs arranged in an L-shaped pattern. A blackboard is on one wall, and a shelf over a sink holds teacups and glasses.

Sagara's charges come to see him after school and on the weekend, usually twice a week altogether. These are junior and senior high school children, mostly from the local area, whose parents have heard of Sagara through word of mouth. Unlike other *juku* (which may have much larger classes), Sagara's does not advertise. The larger, sometimes franchised *juku* have slick brochures that are distributed in the schools; children carry handfuls home with them every week. In Sagara's one-man operation, fees are standard. His classes cost parents about Y18,000 ($84) per month.

Sagara's pupils are headed toward entrance examinations to high school and university. Some children are with Sagara because they've tried other *juku* or tutors and haven't caught fire. No one here is a remedial case; the children are all bright, he says, but some have "attitude" problems or need better study habits.

Toru Shigematsu, fifteen, has been a student of Sagara's for three years. Toru is shy but stubborn. He is very intelligent, but the standards he sets for himself are high and uncompromising, and thus he is often frustrated and unhappy. His perfectionism is a problem, but so is his independence: he insists on working in his own way, at hours which worry his mother (usually 1:00 A.M. to 6:00A.M.), and only on the subjects which interest him. Sagara's job is to find a middle ground for him, realistic goals, and less idiosyncratic means to reach them. Toru needs, in short, to develop regular and steady habits while concurrently working to the best of his ability. And while trying to build Toru's confidence, Sagara also must reduce his parents' anxieties.

Sagara's approach is first to understand the student. He can quickly see the young person's ability level in various subjects, at least as tested, but motivation is harder to grasp. He says it takes six to eight months of observation to get to know a student. In his *juku*, as in the ordinary classroom, the overt assumption is that "all have equal ability," but he, and all teachers, know that "ten children have ten different ability levels." Hence, Sagara's operating premise diverges from the ideal of egalitarian homogeneity that, as a matter of ideology, underlies Japanese education.

Sagara says he knows his charges better than the classroom teacher, who, after all, has over forty pupils to monitor. He says further that his establishment resembles the environment of the traditional *terakoya* (temple school), where the relationship between pupil and teacher was personal. Most *juku*, however, are much larger than Sagara's, making close relationships impossible. In any case, twice a year Sagara schedules long interviews with his students' parents, to evaluate their children's progress and to allow him to judge their involvement.

Sagara feels that the most important qualities for a Japanese child today—"in these hard times," as the Japanese always assert—are a "strong and energetic spirit" and a "wide intellectual grasp." *Juku* like Sagara's can help a child develop confidence, and also bring time and effort to bear on specific weak areas. Sagara says that all the children he teaches want to be there, at least after a while, and really understand that he cares about them.

To work against his students' will and wishes is abhorrent to Sagara. When advising them on future schools, he considers first the wishes of the individual, *then* the person's ability, for he says that *kiryoku* (will) is often strong enough to raise ability, if the goal desired is a reasonable one. Meanwhile, parents and regular school advisors often ignore the young person's wishes.

Talking with students and former students of Sagara's *juku*, I found unanimous praise and warm feeling for the instructor. The students see him as on their side, as uncompromisingly working *with* them, and sometimes even as an ally against their parents. He constantly rewards them, and often provides nurturance in the form of treats and surprises, such as getting them ice cream on a hot day or buying them books as special gifts. Toru even received several comic books from Sagara when the young student was sick, and Sagara offered him a whole set of them if he'd promise to study hard for his high school entrance exam. Sagara's relationship with his students is of the kidding, big-brother sort. Sagara once bet his students on the answer to a very hard problem and said that if he were wrong, he'd cut his hair very short. He was and he did. He is boyish and dresses casually, and the intensity of *juku* study is mitigated by Sagara's cheerful liveliness. His former students show their fondness for the school by returning often, and some even come back to help later students. For the graduates, the *juku* experience seems to have been more meaningful than their time in regular schools, for they say "after I graduated from *juku*. . . ." instead of "after I graduated from junior high. . . ." They all say Sagara is one of the most important people in their lives.

Toru initially came to Sagara accompanied by his mother, a professor at a university in Tokyo. She was distraught over Toru's mixed performance in school. She also suffered from her own sense of inadequacy for being unable to motivate her son. And she basically disapproved of an educational system which forces all children, however eccentrically intelligent, to conform to the same program of study and testing. She wanted to be able to trust her own intuition and to let Toru find his own way to bloom, but the pressure of the educational ladder, the influence of other parents, and warnings from teachers forced her to consider *juku*. The only alternative seemed to her to be to abandon the Japanese system altogether and to send Toru to a university in the United States.

Sagara immediately saw that his first job was to give her confidence in her son. He met with her several times. Toru's father was often away, and in any case did not spend much time with Toru, nor did he feel the anxiety felt by his wife. Sagara wanted to let her know he would make time for her as well as for her son. She says that Sagara "saved her life"—that he helped her to put her son's (and her) problem in perspective and gave her someone to rely and lean on, when she had felt so isolated. (Mothers rarely rely on each other in such cases, and seldom on their husbands, but feel they must bear the burden alone.)

Toru is now in a good, but not the "best" high school, and the whole family says it is through Sagara's efforts and kindness that he made it. Toru's school is about forty-five minutes from his home— by bus and two trains plus a ten-minute walk. It is an older high school, next to a famous shrine, whose open courtyards and precincts are used by the children for sports practice. The graduates of Toru's school attend a wide range of universities, and the principal is proud of the eminence of some of the alumni. Toru still has to work hard, for in two years the examination tension begins again, and he continues to make the biweekly trip to Sagara's *juku.*

THE PERSISTENCE OF HARMONY

Even though a split exists between school and *juku,* the homeroom teacher is still the official center of the moral and social goals of learning, entrusted with the job of training children in correct social behavior: cooperation, sharing, the need to be sensitive to other people's feelings and points of view, and proper respect for elders, especially manifested in correct forms of address. All this is part of the teaching agenda, and is inculcated in members of a small group that spends many months together. In Japan, appropriate social behavior is not held up as a special attribute of well-raised or well-adjusted children. It is instead regarded as something absolutely essential to social harmony—which is to say, to bedrock Japanese morality—and therefore something that all children can and must attain by carefully observing classroom rules and complying with the teacher's usually unobtrusive guidance.

And yet the emphasis on "harmony" in the psychodynamics of learning is not complete and unambiguous. Japanese parents, of course, want the very best for their children, now and in the future, and that means getting the best education for them. In turn, that best education is defined as being admitted to a prestigious university, which is near impossible without *juku.* Parents also hedge their bets by hiring college students as tutors and by employing other aids to study. Particularly anxious and suspicious parents may even ask their children to study alone, to hide study materials from friends lest an "advantage" be lost. This kind of competitive privatizing of education is the subject of much criticism in the press and among professional educators, both of whom blame the problem on selfish parents, especially the too-pushy mother.

For children, however, the experience of secondary education is not necessarily confined to preparing for exams. There is time for friendship as well. In spite of academic pressure, one finds more mutual support than competitive suspiciousness in the Japanese high school. As it was in middle school, the exams do not pit child against child; rather, the child struggles against the institution of the test or against the abstract goal of success in the face of the odds.

Nor are all teachers devoted to preparing young people for the examinations. Japanese teachers believe that if they themselves are not engaged in the subject they teach, they cannot successfully help their students to learn. This much was evident when I observed a mathematics class for second-year high school students in Hiroshima.

The instructor was a young man in his late thirties who began the class by writing on the board for about five minutes without saying anything. The resulting formulas filled the blackboard. Meanwhile, the students chatted, arranged pencils on their desks, and looked out the window. The teacher occupied himself furiously, undistracted by classroom noise.

Suddenly he turned around, his face aglow and his arms waving. He exhorted the class to look at what he had done, saying that it might be hard to see it now, but by the end of the class they would all see how beautiful the math was. He was virtually jumping up and down as he took his students through the formulas. He said, "This is really going to be beautiful! If you take the time and effort to understand it, it will really be worth it, because the beauty will knock you over—I know that there are many different tastes, and many different notions of what beauty is, but I promise you that if you look hard at this, you'll all be pleased."

This teacher is not the exception in Japan. To teach is to share joy with one's students, and by doing so, to motivate them to work hard. The teacher's first and best tool is his or her own emotional involvement.

WHAT IS AN ADOLESCENT?

Japanese children between the ages of thirteen and nineteen have not traditionally been seen as a special age group with a set of special problems. They are not, in our sense of the term, "teenagers." The Western, especially American, preoccupation with the age group has no parallel in Japan. Only recently have Japanese parents and educators begun to worry about "teenage" behavior and attitudes.

As Thomas Rohlen has pointed out,[11] Japanese have no word for "teenager," and high schoolers are most commonly called "children." There are formal Japanese terms for children age seven or eight to fourteen or fifteen, called *shonen,* and age fifteen to twenty-four, *seinen.* But the terms are not in common use colloquially. Even the word "adolescent," which in Western usage denotes a child from the onset of puberty to the end of the teens, has no Japanese-language equivalent. In traditional Japan, apparently, no one saw the need for a word that implied raging glandular development and problematic behavior. Even today, Japanese children of the age group are, on the whole, well integrated into family life, committed at school, and deeply involved in friendships. Accordingly, few are alienated, sociopathic, or self-destructive.

When Western parents fear their children's "rebellious" tendencies, they often do one of two things. They yield to the cry for independence—for peers or solitude rather than family—or they try, sometimes desperately, to impose control. This takes the form of curfews, telephone eavesdropping, and interrogation after returning from a date, all of which is regarded by the teenager as intrusive and humiliating. Parents say they want to protect their children from the vices of the street, but they may also be personally threatened by the images of the teenager thrown up by our culture.

There is, of course, no one tried and true path of child development that has been universally recognized by everyone always and everywhere. The life of the child, like the life of the adult, is variously defined by local cultural assumptions and historical circumstances. Accordingly, Japanese concepts of childhood have changed during the past three hundred years. Chinese understanding of human relationships derived from Confucius, selected and tempered by Japanese convictions about successful discipline and engagement, formed a basis for later Japanese pedagogical ideas.

But, as we know, all Japanese conceptions of child development, including those held today, regard relationships as more important than any set of innate or biologically determined drives. In the end, human relationships amplify or constrain a child's potential. A child, even a teenager, is thus the product of, and sensitive to, the environment provided for him by adults—the child being thoroughly amenable to the influence of those caring for him. Japanese educational theory and the folk psychology of mothers both assert that the child's faults lie not in the stars but in the society that has the power to shape his condition.

So when a Japanese child refuses to study, or "hangs out" with a bad element, or lets his hair grow too long, Japanese adults look to the family or school for causes, and rarely to any deep-seated or age-related psychological problem in the child himself. It is the school's responsibility to occupy the child's classroom hours with purpose and engagement, and it is up to the parents, or to the pressures inflicted by exams, to take up the rest of the child's time.

By tradition, relationships with peers are regarded as important. In the past, however, high schoolers and college students have been especially prone to develop strong "vertical" ties with students younger and older than themselves. These *sempai/kohai* (senior/junior) relationships often last a lifetime. The elder helps the younger get a job or find a likely mate, and otherwise smoothes the path, with the younger doing errands for and offering devotion to the elder. Recently, however, the young seem increasingly to associate with those of the same age, thanks to limitations on the time available for participation in clubs and other activities that bring together people of different ages.

A recent crossnational study of high schoolers shows some interesting divergences between Japanese and American students.[12] First, Japanese children in school most often associate with their friends, who are mostly of the same sex. American students prefer friends of the opposite sex, and see them most often outside school. The Japanese child's greatest interest in school lies in mastering academic subjects, while the American student most enjoys extracurricular activities. Japanese children say that extracurricular activities are important because they strengthen friendships, while American counterparts say they help one's chances of getting into a good college. Japanese children say that the most important thing in their lives is study, while American students say it is sex—or at least romantic attachment. American students say that their parents are not proud of them, while Japanese children say that their parents love them unconditionally and are proud of them too, simply because, as one put it, "I am their own child."

WHAT DO THEY DO BESIDES STUDY?

Japanese adults think that Japanese teenagers have too much free time. So mothers, educators, and city officials go about trying to find ways to fill it productively. But on Sunday, Japanese teenagers are often left to their own devices, and they look most like their American counterparts (although to us oddly innocent) as they meet for coffee, ice cream, or shopping in the "young" areas of their town or city—if Tokyo, in Shibuya or Harajuku. Those who have left school after high school or junior high may have some money to spend, especially if they live at home, because few contribute to maintaining the household. For many children, Sundays may mean *juku* or study. Yet the most well known Sunday street scene is one of young people, watching each other and street dancing in Tokyo's Harajuku. Or they might be strolling through T-shirt boutiques, buying plastic earrings and other non-dress-code-approved accessories worn only on such occasions. Of course, even in "rebellion" the dancers observe the patterns of mainstream society. They arrive in discrete groups, each known by its own costume; later they will change back into everyday clothes, sometimes even into their school uniforms, for the trip home at the end of the day. Some think that the Harajuku Sunday is the beginning of the end of Japanese society. But like so many Japanese phenomena that permit that coexistence of anomalies and homogeneity, street dancing releases pressure and thereby protects, not rends, the social fabric.

Other forms of "antisocial" behavior among Japanese teenagers include the reading of *manga,* or comic books. These are often nearly wordless and full of violence. A typical high school student may go through two or three of the 350-page books a week. *Manga* are part of a huge industry, including the manufacture of a wide array of things bearing the images of popular characters, who, like other "stars," may also be used in ad campaigns to hawk beer and other consumer products. The use of stickers with the characters on them is forbidden in school, but children get around the code by concealing them inside a bag or jacket.

The Japanese high school student spends very little time with his family. When at home, he is most often watching television, studying, or sleeping. Roused by his mother early, he bolts down breakfast and pores over his lessons before running for the bus or train. He may return home briefly between school and *juku,* if he attends one, and finally returns at the end of the day around 6:00 P.M. He may fall asleep before dinner, in which case his mother will simply make his dinner later when he awakes, sometimes at 10:00 P.M.—when his father returns. Then, after watching some television, the teenager often sets his alarm for the small hours of the morning for study until breakfast. The high schooler's time, except for school and *juku,* is his alone to determine, and his family makes no special demands and imposes no schedule. Even on weekends, he will spend his free time away from home with his friends. The unity of the contemporary Japanese family thus includes only younger children, and simply provides a nurturant pit-stop for the otherwise self- and school-determined lives of teenagers.

Differences are now growing between secondary school boys and girls in their experiences and in the expectations adults have for them. Boys are typically allowed more freedom to hang out with their peers; girls are more likely to be required to keep "proper" hours and are not allowed to associate with "improper" friends. As mentioned previously, girls are usually not exhorted to study as hard as boys, and fewer family resources are likely to be expended in *juku* and other forms of academic help for them. Although many parents hope that their daughters will attend college, the time spent there is seen to qualify the young women for a good marriage rather than for a good job and independent financial security. Moreover, entrance to "too good" a coeducational university might easily hurt a girl's chances of getting an appropriate husband. Girls who enter Tokyo University (Todai), the pinnacle of academic success, may find themselves completely ineligible for marriage, because Tokyo University males (and all others) prefer to marry presumably less independent women from a less exalted institution.

Two High School Seniors

To flesh out the generalizations in this chapter about the lives of Japanese secondary school students, two portraits will be given of individuals in their third year of high school. The first portrait provides an example of a young person who is not on a track to a prestigious university and whose parents are not putting great pressure on him to work very hard. The second portrait shows a young man who, pushed by his family, is bending all his energies to make it to the top.

Yukio: A Normal but Not Normative Youth

Yukio is a senior in a public high school in Sendai, a provincial city in northeast Japan. Harold Stevenson,[13] having compared the social attitudes and performances of schoolchildren, has said that Sendai resembles Minneapolis in its class structure, its generally middle-class nature, and its cultural "centrality": it is mid-Japan, just as Minneapolis is "mid-America."

Yukio's father, a technician in an automobile plant, had only a high school education, as did his mother. The two have three children: Yukio, the eldest, and two daughters, aged fifteen and twelve, both in junior high school. The fifteen-year-old, very interested in music, takes violin lessons after school twice a week, while the other daughter seems to be more interested in sports than in school or the arts. Yukio has been enrolled in a *juku* for the last year, but before that had no outside classes or lessons of any kind.

Yukio is what his teachers call an "all-around boy." He enjoys ice-skating and swimming, sings in a chorus (his major school club activity), and otherwise enjoys hanging out with his friends—or did enjoy it until most of their time was eroded by lessons and cram classes in preparation for the examinations. Yukio wants to go to college, but isn't highly motivated to attend a prestigious liberal arts school. He'd rather go to a technical school, where there is less entrance pressure, and sees himself more or less following in his father's footsteps.

His mother hopes he might go to a college that would give him a chance at a managerial job, but she doesn't push him very hard, worrying that she might alienate him if she does. He has been very clear that he won't be pushed, and has, she feels, deliberately dug in his heels against her. She continues to help him with his studies and to encourage him, and has had several talks with his teachers and with the guidance counselor at his school, hoping that perhaps someone else might have more influence over him. His teachers see him as a mediocre student, willing to study only if he is interested in something, but a little lazy (or resistant) if he is not. They feel that to push him to aspire to a major university would be useless.

Yukio has separated himself, over the past year, from those of his friends who aspire to such schools, although they were the students with whom he used to be closest. He feels that he is now on a different track, and the intensity and isolation of their lives at the moment makes them unavailable to him in any case. On the other hand, he doesn't associate with classmates who are on the edge of "dropping out." Very bright and in no way alienated from study, he is simply not willing to push himself farther than his interests might lead him; he is not interested in hard work for its own sake or in the credentials that a top university might confer upon him. He knows that some of his teachers think he is lazy, but he is not concerned about that: his math teacher is an ally, and knows that when he wants to apply himself, he is extremely capable—math is his best subject.

Yukio's father had moved to the city to attend a technical school, but dropped out to take a job when Yukio's grandparents needed money, working hard ever since to gain expertise and seniority. Having stayed with the same company for twenty-five years, he has reached the top of his blue-collar track. He is also a leader in the company union and a liaison to management. Every spring, just before the annual union "spring offensive," Yukio's father becomes intensely involved in negotiations for the next year's salary levels and other bargaining points, and the family often doesn't really see him for several weeks.

With his own room, Yukio closets himself there after school, listening to his stereo on earphones until it is time to go to *juku*. After he comes home, he has a late supper, and watches television if his mother has not persuaded him to study. His father likes to go fishing or to a ball game with him on Sundays. Yukio doesn't spend a lot of time with his sisters, and instead goes to movies or to coffee shops with his current two best friends, who, like him, neither aspire to the top nor have dropped out. One is mechanically inclined, the other likes to write but doesn't do well in school. The first comes from a blue-collar family like Yukio's, and the second is the second son of a woman whose husband, a lower-level executive in an insurance company, left her five years ago. This boy works after school to help out at home, and spends the rest of his time either writing or amusing himself with his two friends.

Yukio's school day begins with a homeroom class meeting. He has no special interest in talk of the upcoming library day or the yearbook committee, and perks up only when the sports day (*taiikusai*) is brought up. This is a ritualized but highly engaging annual episode in the life of the school, which involves everyone, including teachers, staff, and even the P-TA. The form of the pervasive activity differs slightly from school to school. In elementary grades, it is called *undokai*.

Yukio's entire school is divided into four teams, known by their different-colored caps. The teams take part in various kinds of events in which the competition occurs between teams and not between individuals. In elementary schools hurdle jumping, footraces, broad jumps, and relay races culminate in a giant tug-of-war, in which the entire red team takes on the entire white team. Many of the games are similar to the "new games," considered cooperative efforts, that became popular in the 1970s in the United States. One such individually noncompetitive event is the giant ball game, in which a huge inflated sphere is passed overhead, from one set of hands to another, over a long line made up of all the children on a team. The first team to complete the pass successfully wins. Throughout, children are not singled out for attention: there are no champions or most valuable players, except as informally noted by classmates. If there is a winner, a team is cheered, not a person.

Although high school sports days are not as formal as the *undokai* of the elementary school, being intended more for entertainment, Yukio takes them seriously. His class's representative to the sports day organizing committee, he works with two other students to assign various tasks. As seniors, his class is expected to act as referees, measurers, and record keepers, as well as coordinators of the spoofs and skits developed by students. He fills in the class on the progress of his committee as well as reporting to the schoolwide committee. His "tour of duty" will end after the meet, and he looks forward to it as his moment of glory: as the leader of the seniors that day, he will be regarded as the leader of the school.

In spite of the intensity of preparing for the examination, and the isolation of those studying the hardest, high school still remains a place of cohesion rather than competition, of support rather than anomie. Yukio is already saddened by the prospect of leaving, and becomes sentimental even about teachers he didn't like, about class trips, and especially about concerts his chorus has performed. He even begins to envy those students who are cramming for the exams, since they are part of a process that calls for a most compelling and identity-conferring effort; marginal to it, he has no need to look ahead to the crescendo of application and its satisfaction and resolution. His will come during the sports day, and that will be soon over.

There are several keys here to the high school experience in Japan. First, Yukio is not on the elite university track so often described in accounts of the Japanese educational experience. Thus, we see the elite course from an outsider's perspective. We also see that other educational options exist; in fact, most students are more like Yukio than like those comparatively few struggling to get into prestigious universities.

Second, it is indeed hard to be both "all-around" and to get first-rate educational credentials in Japan. The educational ideology espouses the idea of the "whole child," but by Yukio's age some choices have to be made. Yukio is obviously an academically talented youngster, at least in mathematics, but he wants little to do with the high school fast track. Although not academically alienated, neither is he intensely committed to "getting ahead" using the academic system. Also, he is interested in music and sports but does not want a career in either.

The Normative Dream: Nobuya on the Path to Todai

Unlike Yukio, Nobuya has a very clear sense of direction. He is now a junior at a very prestigious high school in Tokyo, having earlier passed several critical hurdles. He's been in *juku* since the fifth grade. Nobuya's uncle on his mother's side went to Tokyo University, although not in the law department, which bears the greatest prestige. His father attended Nagoya University before moving to Tokyo to work for Mitsubishi Heavy Industries.

Nobuya has a younger sister who is a junior high school student. She does not attend an academic *juku,* but plays the piano organ, receiving weekly group lessons in the neighborhood. The parents hope she will go to a two-year junior college, although she wants to attend a four-year institution. In any case, the family is unable at this time to pay for more instruction because Nobuya's expenses are high. In addition to *juku* classes twice a week, Nobuya has a home tutor once a week to work on mathematics. The tutor is a third-year student at Tokyo University whose mother is a friend of Nobuya's mother.

The impetus for Tokyo University seems to have come wholly from Nobuya's mother's family. His uncle, convinced that he would be an appropriate candidate, actively encourages him. There is no acknowledged "back door" to Tokyo University through which an applicant can enter via bribery or influence. But because the uncle took him on a tour of the two campuses of Todai, introducing him informally to his former teachers, Nobuya's family has a feeling of "connection" to the university.

Nobuya is, according to his teachers, a reasonably bright boy, not exceptional in any area but very serious and hardworking. He has no gang of friends, preferring to be close to one boy; in any case, Nobuya's schedule keeps him from any form of leisurely socializing. He doesn't enjoy sports, nor does he have any hobbies, though he does play chess with his father and watch television.

Nobuya's life is shaped by school, *juku,* tutoring, and the Sunday practice tests that he takes at a cram school in central Tokyo. Family vacations and quick excursions are no longer taken. Even at New Year's, the most compelling holiday on the Japanese calendar, Nobuya will be at *juku,* at a symbolic gathering aimed at confirming students' sense of self-sacrifice and mobilization toward the examinations.

His teachers predict (but with great hesitation, as if the evil eye might be attracted by optimism) that Nobuya will get into Tokyo University. In his case, what will make the difference is his willingness to work hard, to accede to his mother's supportive encouragement. His teachers (and parents, occasionally) regret the narrowness of his life, noting that he is almost "too smooth," with no interesting "edges" to his personality, no resistance to the influences that are directing him. But, they say, there will be time to develop his interests and personality in college, where he can work or relax as he wants to, and where his schedule will be his own.

NOBUYA AND YUKIO COMPARED

Nobuya's life gives us a view of the most valued ladder of success furnished by the school system. This path, a liberal arts–oriented academic one, precludes choosing a "technical" or "vocational" track, which is not an elite or even mainstream course. School reformers are attempting now to provide students with various ladders and to return streaming by interests and abilities. But the strongly egalitarian ideology that imbues educational debate, thanks especially to the Teachers' Union's platforms, has so far prevented the any reform: the dream of Tokyo University must remain "available" to all.

Unlike Nobuya, whose skills seem evenly distributed, Yukio has shown strong academic talent in mathematics and has not been encouraged to develop evenly in all areas. The structure and distribution of time in secondary schools, however, may prevent students like Yukio from displaying and energetically spending time to develop an aptitude. In Japan specialization in itself is seen as a problem, and like the technician, the specialist finds himself compartmentalized and kept from moving up to top-level jobs. Companies prefer to hire new recruits with no speciality and to train them to the particular skills they need—usually a broad range of skills, which will give a recruit the special flavor and culture of the hiring company. Again, it's a matter of the "way we do it."

Another point to remember in summing up the Japanese secondary school experience is that while effort and struggle are valued there, competition between students most definitely is not. The competitive striving that is to be avoided in regular school is exhibited, if at all, in the *juku* or *yobiko*. This means that the regular classroom is a place where harmony must prevail. The annual sports day, a hymn to group effort and team play, not individual competition, symbolizes the most valued forms of incentive offered to children. It is important to remember that even where a sense of the competitive is an active part of the Japanese educational environment, the form that it takes does not pit an individual child against another or all others, but rather against an agreed-upon set of external standards that demand a high level of performance.

Where children in *juku* or in regular school are mobilized by teachers and even peers to cram, this activity is, oddly enough, and as we have noted, another Japanese way to create group feeling and cohesion, rather than division and separation. Yet the Japanese high school student today is perhaps more isolated than his or her prewar counterpart, more given to the solitary activity of cramming facts into his head. Today clubs and other social activities provide less communal solace. Nevertheless, the extent of the isolation, except for a few cases of tragic distortion, is far less pervasive than the publicity and stereotypes might lead us to believe. Nobuya does enjoy going to *juku,* and, although he likes to sleep late, does not groan too much when his mother awakens him early on Sundays to attend the test sessions.

In any case, the Japanese high school student, unlike his American counterpart, is still a protected child—still seen as in need of care and support, of direction and indulgence—all of which our youths would reject.

To return to the writer of the letter to "Beth." The teenager already sees herself as a negotiator on her own behalf, a person with rights and entitlement, whose academic performance is her own business. She wants some respect and self-determination, and most of all wants her "privileges" left alone. She sees no need to study for the sake of study, nor even the need to earn the privileges she covets through academic endeavor. School being something adults do to children, she is wriggling like an insect on a pin to free herself of the dominance that situation implies. Independence, taught to her early, seems to contradict the messages she now gets that she in fact cannot choose for herself if she makes the wrong choices. Indignant at the mixed messages she has received, she rejects the idea that she still is a child with a lot to learn. For the Japanese high school student, in contrast, independence and freedom of choice are not primary goals of socialization. Hence, he is for the most part wholeheartedly engaged in acquiring what he thinks he needs, and what society insists that he needs, to succeed later in life.

PART III

NATIONAL NEEDS AND LOCAL GOALS

Education in Modern Societies

9

JAPAN IN TRANSITION

Nostalgia and Reform in a Postindustrial Society

How do the Japanese view their schools today? What do Japanese parents, teachers, and policymakers think about the environment in which children grow up? Is it paradise or hell or compromise? What do they hope for and how would they reform their schools?

It is above all clear that whatever the success of the Japanese school in turning out children who learn more and better than children elsewhere, Japanese parents are far from satisfied with their educational system. In a recent survey[1] mothers in Minneapolis and Sendai were asked to evaluate their children's school experiences. The Minneapolis mothers consistently answered queries by saying that the schools were fine and that their children were doing well. However, the Sendai mothers, very critical of their schools, were worried that their children were not performing up to potential. Whose children were, in objective tests, doing better? The Sendai group—in fact, so much better that the poorest performer in some classes in the Japanese group was well ahead of the best in comparable classes in the American group.

Of course, criticism itself has meanings and uses in Japan that are different from those of the West. Japanese "self-effacement"—which contains elements of both sincere modesty and a self-protective low profile—may account for some of the complaints against the schools, especially when the Japanese talk to foreign observers. To them, Japanese parents and educators often praise Western education for its "creativity" and its "attention to the individual," but many Japanese I interviewed confined themselves to saying "I wish our children had as much free time as yours."

The Japanese do recognize strengths in their schools, especially the primary schools, and few are eager to exchange systems wholesale. Like middle-class liberal American parents who want to send their children to public schools but do not, because they live in districts where they feel the schools are substandard, Japanese parents do not want to risk their own children's future by sacrificing it to sentimental parental ideals. The American parents either move to suburbs where there are good schools or put their children into expensive private schools, abandoning the cherished "neighborhood school" altogether; the Japanese parents fully participate in the examination struggle, even though they don't want to chain their children to eternal study. An overwhelming majority of Japanese mothers give up their own chances for a career or for outside employment during the years their children are in school, to spend time helping them with schoolwork or simply to be there when needed. To do otherwise is risky, both for the child and for the mother's reputation. A mother who worked as an airlines representative during her child's early years quit suddenly when her child's grades slipped a little. She felt that his problem was her selfishness—continuing to work—which showed a lack of motherly dedication and effort.

As Thomas Rohlen has described the problem:

> A division arises here between public values and private interests, between idealism and reality. The public, idealistic goals remain central to the rhetoric of politicians, officials, teachers, parents and students. And they are all sincere in their desire that education furthers the development of democracy and promotes individual growth. Yet, when the chips are down, most parents want success for their own children more than anything else. A gap thus develops between parents and educators, one that has great significance to the question of reform.[2]

Japanese parents and educators both, however, encourage a national debate over what is good for children—a debate that draws heated attention from people of all persuasions and constituencies. Education, in public opinion polls across Japan, is *the* primary topic of concern for the great majority of adults. One of the most significant elements of the public discussion is: what is missing in the experience of childhood, and what is the responsibility of the educational system to provide the absent elements?

The Good Old Days

The look back has always given a nostalgic tone to Japanese public debate. The recent astonishing success of the book *Totto-chan: The Little Girl at the Window,* by Tetsuko Kuroyanagi,[3] has been attributed to its intensely sweet reminiscences of a happy childhood spent in a prewar school. The book sold over 6 million copies. The school's fictive principal, Mr. Sosaku Kobayashi, would admonish the parents and teachers of his charges, "Leave them to nature. . . . Don't cramp their ambitions. Their dreams are bigger than yours." The warmth of the school—which physically was housed in a circle of railroad cars, and which featured impromptu pajama parties, long walks in the country, and emphasis on empathy and self-development— captured the imagination of Japanese readers. Why? Because they would like to escape the pressure their own real-world children are experiencing. But the memories of those with quite different "reformist" perspectives were also catalyzed: elements of prewar education of the more ordinary sort became part of the discourse as well. The two reactions to *Totto-chan* represent the perspectives of the major reform movements in Japan.

The first—the call for a natural, Rousseauistic environment in which a child's free spirit may develop—is redolent of the 1920s, when John Dewey's influence was strong in Japan. "Free schools" and other manifestations of the movement were then evident, and revived for a while after the war. Recently, there has been some intellectual interest in "de-schooling," but few applications of the idea have caught on. Meanwhile, nurturant attention to a child's disposition has persisted and even flourished in the preschools and in elementary schools, but the self-direction and permissiveness of Totto's school is scarcely found.

As an example of the school's mood, Totto recalls a time when she dropped her purse into the outdoor privy and began to shovel its contents out to look for her bag. She had produced a large evil-smelling pile when the principal walked by and asked her what she was doing, and then simply walked on, saying mildly, "You'll put it all back when you've finished, won't you?"

Totto-chan's school represents another form of tolerance, not just for behavioral eccentricities, but for differentness of a more visible and permanent sort—something that has always represented a major personal and social problem in Japan. Totto-chan tells of her special friendships with a boy handicapped by polio and with a dwarfed child, both of whom were treated like ordinary children at her school. Japanese readers are well aware of the double handicap such children suffer in a society where by tradition differentness is to be covered up and where in the past children with severe handicaps were not educated but were hidden as "the family's shame."

The best-seller's theme is the love and care that the school lavishes on the children, rather than the children's development as individuals— the latter being something a Western reader might expect. The "free school" in Japan is a place where the teachers are free to love and understand the children, an ideal that in fact also applies to more traditional schools.

Current sentiment extols the good qualities of more orthodox prewar schools as well. The relationship between teacher and student was said to be closer and more permanent, the student's loyalty to the school deeper, and the child's life more balanced and dedicated. Like Totto-chan, present-day adults remember youthful pranks as evidence of the luxury of leisure they possessed, and as evidence also of the existence of "appropriate" childhood activities involving peers. And these adults feel that modern schools lack a moral core, a sense of purpose—what the Japanese call an *ikigai,* or "reason for living."

A Search for Life Goals

This word, *ikigai,* appears frequently in discussions of Japanese childhood and schooling. A common term in Japanese folk psychology, its meaning can range from "significant pastime" to a more deeply philosophic "life goal." Japanese value *ikigai* as a motivating premise for life at all levels, and even a housewife's commitment to her neighborhood literary group is seen as completely legitimate and significant.

Contemporary schools are not providing *ikigai* for children, it is said, and education is geared to examinations, which are ironically regarded to offer a reason not for living but for dying. By analogy, the call for restoration of *ikigai* in schools corresponds to the call by the American organization Moral Majority for rejuvenation of moral standards and principles, prayer in the schools, order in the hallways, and respect for the flag.

Japanese nostalgia sometimes takes in prewar nationalism, because the reformers were raised in the prewar period that forms the point of reference. And some of the fervor they now find missing was indeed related to military mobilization—a fervor which they felt, but may not have understood, as children. Even those old enough to understand that they, too, were part of a war effort were later to remember more the feeling of engagement, and less the rhetoric and nationalistic propaganda that moved adults at the time.

A new sort of nationalism pervades the calls for the restoration of moral instruction in schools. This is closely tied to both the confidence Japan has developed since the economic boom of the 1960s and to the insecurities of trade war politics and the awareness of resource scarcity highlighted by the oil shock of the early 1970s.

Japanese social critics point to the treatment of World War II in high school textbooks as an example of the dangerous inroads made by Japanese nationalism. Recently textbooks approved by the ministry of education have been criticized for turning a blind eye to Japanese aggression during World War II, and for a biased interpretation of Japanese actions in China before the war. A commemoration of the fortieth anniversary of the bombing of Hiroshima and Nagasaki in August 1985 produced a raft of criticism against textbooks that referred to the Japanese only as victims of the bomb, not as full-scale participants in a world war. Such lapses in textbooks may or may not represent a form of nationalism that had earlier led Japan into World War II. But many Japanese feel that to raise children who have a less than balanced view of the war years is bad, and perhaps dangerous.

On the whole, however, the ''new nationalism'' seems most typically expressed in a higher international profile for Japan, a new confidence in the nation's economic stature, and, at least in some ways, a greater sense of responsibility for aiding less advanced countries. Compared to the very low profile earlier assumed by Japan, this new nationalism appears very bold indeed.

THE MINISTRY OF EDUCATION: ROLE AND REFORM

The ministry of education is responsible for the uniform content and even distribution of educational resources across the population.

Because the ministry itself has not been central to elite political concerns, and because, overall, the Japanese educational system has met the needs of its most critical constituent—employers and employees—there has been little pressure to innovate radically. Accordingly, the ministry has a deserved reputation for conservatism in the content and administration of education. Moreover, the ministry is itself not seen as a place to work for those who want a high-status government career. There are, of course, many extremely well qualified and hardworking bureaucrats in the ministry, but it does not attract the most creative or ambitious graduates of the elite universities.

In any case, the ministry of education directs curricula, approves textbooks, and generally supervises all aspects of education. Other functions include the drafting of bills and preparation of the budget for the Diet, the establishment and direction of surveys and research institutes, and the supervision of museums and grants related to culture and education. Under the minister, who is a political appointee, and his advisors there are five bureaus: elementary and secondary education, higher education, social (adult) education, physical education, and administration.

The most important advisory committee is the Liberal Democratic party's Education Committee, on which all previous ministers, and many senior Diet members, sit. The committee is regarded as a powerful conservative influence on Japanese education.

Critics of the educational system point to the fact that centralization has kept teachers and schools from innovating. Critics also say that the educational system provides a single-model path to mainstream, generalist careers—the role and life of a white-collar worker in a large company, a "Mitsubishi man" or a member of the "Itoh team." Personal differences and options other than those ordained by the path are not considered completely legitimate, even if they are not explicitly discouraged.

The major public role of the ministry is as a participant in the stand-off debate with the Teachers' Union, which continually opposes what it regards as the educational establishment. But the union has so far been only an irritant and counterfoil in the educational debate, not a source of new proposals.

While the Japan Teachers' Union and others want to protect the reforms effected by the Occupation—egalitarianism and universal education—the ministry and Liberal Democratic party are the "reformers," hoping to "re-Japanize" Japanese education. In short, the "liberals" want to conserve the system, while the "conservatives" want to change it.

THE PRIME MINISTER'S COMMITTEE

In 1985 Prime Minister Nakasone established an ad hoc Committee on Educational Reform to look into Japanese education and develop a set of ideas for improving it. The political implication of Nakasone's decision was evident from the beginning, and the usual hue and cry was heard in the columns of social commentators, in letters to the editors, and in academic circles. Although the committee has not—as of this writing—produced more than preliminary statements, several issues in ensuing public discussions have emerged as critical.

Some of the issues are: tracking in secondary schools, the system of examinations, the restructuring of secondary education, improving the environments in schools to enhance creativity and individual development, and fostering an international view and capabilities in children.

Tracking

As we have seen, the Japanese school, influenced by a traditional cultural bias against making distinctions between children and by the egalitarian position of the Teachers' Union, avoids overt tracking of students by ability. In current discussions, however, there is some indication that the implicit distinctions that are observable between children in classes and between schools will be made explicit. Teachers themselves admit that it is hard to preserve "harmony" in a class in which some children are nearly illiterate and others have skills that have been honed by outside instruction.

Obviously, because of the pyramidal shape of status in both Japanese education and employment, the "better" the school or job, the fewer opportunities there are to win a place at the top. The most restrictive view has it that success comes only through a Tokyo University degree, only from its law department, and only by assuming a Class I position in the ministry of finance. Given that, training for other ways of making a living is necessarily ranked lower; yet, because of the egalitarian and meritocratic ideal of the Japanese educational system, a definite stigma is placed on anything that early on smacks of reducing a child's chances to climb to the very top. Thus vocational education, though it has existed in various forms in traditional and modern Japan, has in no way become part of the middle-class ideal that has governed the assumptions and modes of the educational mainstream. Vocational education, present in the Tokugawa period as craft and trade apprenticeships, took a modern industrial form in the early years of the Meiji period as training programs at shipyards. Throughout modernization, however, Japan has favored general over technical education. This perpetuates some of the prejudice against manual labor held by the Chinese elites from whom Japan's first formal educational hierarchies were borrowed, while, unlike the Chinese model, the self-made man who is unafraid of getting his hands dirty is also a folk hero in Japan.

The current discussion about reform supports a more realistic view of children's options and abilities and the responsibility of society to provide every child with a culturally valued career. Furthermore, diversifying the curriculum will allow children to choose programs that suit their interests and predilections.

The Examinations

The examinations are the most dramatic and visible object of potential reform. The exam system assumes that distinctions in children's ability to mobilize effort can be measured by a single test; it is further assumed the exams serve the meritocratic, egalitarian ideals of modern Japan. But the existence of the exams, and the increasing number of children who at younger and younger ages sit for them, have produced an explosion of intense anxiety.

The increase in the *juku* industry, the ubiquitous tutoring, and the diminution of family life and leisure with peers in service to the preparation for exams are given as evidence that the examinations must be deemphasized if not removed. In this view, *juku* are seen as a parasitic phenomenon that threatens to smother education with competitive desperation. Yet attempts to abolish or even play down the practical importance of *juku* have consistently failed.

The Restructuring of Secondary Education

The examinations are tied to the current 6–3–3–4 system, a holdover from Occupation reforms. The separation of the three-year high school from the years of compulsory schooling has become demographically obsolete, since nearly all junior high school students go on to high school.

If, as some reformers hope, high school can become part of the compulsory system, there will be much less pressure on junior high school students who currently have to take tests to enter high school. Distinctions between high schools will of course remain, but passage into them will resemble entrance into junior high schools, and may be determined by lottery or neighborhood, or other ''more egalitarian'' means.

Creativity and Individualism

As noted earlier, ''creativity'' is a term defined by culture, and Japanese observers who think that Western education provides rich opportunities for creative talent to bloom are perhaps indulging in wishful overstatement. In any case, they ignore the creative advantage provided by elementary education, at least, in Japan. How reformers propose to change schooling to direct it toward greater creativity is still unclear. It is evident, however, that the presumed link between creativity and individualism, a particularly Western notion, is the basis of their critique.

The International View

The ''internationalization'' of the Japanese child's world view has been a topic of interest for educators for several decades. Battling Japan's historical and cultural insularity has been an uphill task, since the only valued view of the outside, at least within the current curriculum, is that provided by the schools in a well-organized but ethnocentric course of study.

Hiroshi Kida, the director of Japan's Society for the Promotion of Science and former director of the National Institute for Educational Research, has summarized the issue of internationalization: the creation of children who know how to work productively with foreign counterparts. To do this, he says, they must be individuals:

> It is important to educate a new generation of children to be individual persons, rather than to cooperate with a group. The group model for work

was excellent for *catching up,* but from now on, Japan's leadership in international interdependency is more important, and for this we need *individuals* who can work with other than homogeneous units. We need to create individuals who can bridge the gap.[4]

The issues at hand are, of course, treated differently by various groups within Japan. The national government perceives the problem of tracking as one connected with the problem of maintaining high levels of ability in certain vital fields, especially in technology; the government wants to maintain motivation and incentive for students on several tracks, not all of them leading to the most prestigious jobs. They worry about "keeping the workers happy" while denying them access to that summum bonum of Japanese life, a secure managerial position in a large corporation. To others, the problem of tracking comes down to what Ikuo Amano calls "a crisis of aspiration originating in the overstructuration of society."[5] Amano feels that postindustrial Japanese society is flawed because the corporate and other hierarchies that produced a high level of competitive effort during a period of rapid expansion are now stagnant and merely reproducing themselves. Put another way, the tightly structured relationship between the hierarchies means that creative use of talent is not possible.

On the other hand, Hiroshi Kida is not so much interested in the macrosocial structures as in the coming psychosocial adaptation individuals must make. Unlike Amano, who sees Japan as still vertically organized, Kida sees a shift from the "horizontal" group model to the Western, individualistic mode. This, he says, has important consequences for Japanese education, which should adapt. What a child needs in Kida's new Japan is a flexible, portable identity and set of skills; he must be a person who carries his credentials and abilities with him, not needing to depend on his social nexuses to give him his identity.

Kida's child should be able to move smoothly between national cultures, without impediment or stigma, and should possess fluency in more than the Japanese language. Several years ago, in the mid-1970s, Michio Nagai, who was then minister of education, attempted to internationalize Japanese education. At the time, Japan was recovering from the first "oil shock," and the realization of Japan's dependency on external sources of energy gave a special impetus to the movement. However, the insularity and ethnocentricity of Japanese corporate life and the inertia of the bureaucracy of the ministry of education forestalled any genuine change. The topic, however, is a popular one and reemerges periodically, especially among educators and social commentators who have lived or traveled overseas. These people usually dwell on an abstract need for "international" children, rather than on any personal benefits to be gained from mastering a foreign language or other cosmopolitan skills.

There is one group of children whose experiences cast a particularly ironic light on the subject: the returnee children, or *kikoku shijo*. These children—whose parents have been posted abroad by their companies, banks, or ministries (or have worked for foreign companies outside Japan)—have returned to Japan to complete their education. The children, whether they have had a year in a foreign school or as many as five, most often experience much greater "culture shock" upon returning to Japan than they did on arriving in their foreign host country.

First, the children return to discover that their foreign language skills are not valued—in fact, often quite the contrary. The languages taught in Japanese schools, such as English and French, are taught as subjects for exam taking, not as a way communicate with others. So the returnee's conversational fluency may earn him the epithet "foreigner," or he may be later treated as an *eigoya*, a "seller of English." Second, the child's absence from Japanese schools is seen as a clear handicap, for not only has he lost ground academically, but he is perceived to have lost his "Japanese common sense": as defined earlier, the sociocultural forms, behaviors, and morality appropriate to Japanese society. The child doesn't know the right way to do morning exercises or may have forgotten how to bow appropriately. He may also look different, at least at first, wearing foreign clothes or carrying a foreign knapsack instead of a regulation Japanese bookpack; perhaps he is tanned from living in the tropics.

Rather than trying to harness whatever talents and skills the children may have acquired overseas, the ministry of education and the foreign ministry have responded to the anxieties of parents by establishing "reentry" programs: classes and schools to "reintegrate" these children to Japanese life. So, while talk of reform insists on the importance of global views and skills for Japanese children, the stigma attached to cosmopolitanism continues to plague the "accidental" international child.

FAMILY CHANGE

Educational commentators almost always refer to the home as well as the school as a place for potential reform. Many assert that the intensity of the mother's relationship to her child is a key factor behind the tensions surrounding school achievement. The closeness of the mother and child, reinforced by the father's absence, yields either to doting or to overprotection. In the first instance, the mother submits to the child and offers total indulgence, and in the latter, the mother dominates the child, controlling every aspect of his life. Furthermore, since families live in small, isolated units, the child has little opportunity to become close to other adults. There has been a steady decline in the rate of traditional three-generation households, which is now at about 20 percent of all households. Those that do exist are based on a new model, in which grandparents defer to the rule of the daughter-in-law, and the reciprocal respect and love which (ideally, at least) used to govern intergenerational relationships has been replaced by one-way indulgence from the grandparents.

The child has little time to develop informal peer groups, and so adult culture, not children's culture, pervades the child's experience. Until recently, it is said, children congregated in their neighborhoods in vertically organized, mixed-age friendship groups, which permitted support and learning from a diversity of acquaintances. Children now mix only with their age-mates, and only incidentally, perhaps on the way to and from school and *juku*. Nobuya, the young person headed toward Tokyo University, has no group of friends with whom he "hangs out."

WHAT DO TEACHERS SAY?

While not all teachers participate actively in the Teachers' Union, the concerns of teachers are represented within the spectrum of opinion associated with the union. The most vocal elements are the more radical, advocating drastic reform in the structure and content of education. The more moderate teachers hope for reduced pressure from examinations, safety in schools, and other changes that might contribute to a better atmosphere for teaching and teachers.

Teachers also want smaller class size, not for purposes of "control," but so that they can give individual children more attention. And they would like to have more flexibility within the curriculum— so they can deviate in content and can go at a pace appropriate to their students. As it is, many do not finish the prescribed curriculum at all. Teachers note that the wide discrepancy between the abilities of students means that they must teach at a simple level, to engage the lowest-achieving segment of the class.

At the same time, teachers feel pressure from parents who expect that the school will give their child an edge. If all it takes is effort, and if effort is created by motivation in the classroom, then the life chances of any child are seen to depend on a teacher's ability to get emotional commitment from that child. While precisely this engagement can indeed be seen in the earlier years of schooling, by the latter part of junior high the sense of involvement has been eroded in some schools by pressures coming from outside the classroom. Finally, teachers, especially secondary school teachers, are frightened by the potential for violence in the school; the published data on violent incidents seems minimal, but teachers know that actual numbers are somewhat higher and that preventive or ameliorative measures have not been forthcoming.

Parents Call for Change

Parents and teachers rarely speak in abstractions about the various broad positions for change that influence the felt need for educational reform. While the rhetoric is available to them in the media, published reports, and official statements, local P-TA meetings address very concrete problems. How parents interpret the problems is often influenced by the media—*ijime* (bullying) is an example—but few parents speak the language of national commentators.

When parents ask for change, they do so tentatively, and, as I have said, they are unwilling to risk their own children's future by striking out on unorthodox paths. In general, parents want to deemphasize the exams, especially at the junior high school level, and hope that the need for expensive *juku* and private tutoring will drop off the face of the earth. They are worried most immediately about violence in the schools, and want to protect their children from physical abuse. Finally, they hope their children will *want* to do well and not need to struggle too hard; yet if anyone has to push their children, they would rather the teachers do it, not themselves.

Meanwhile, very few Japanese parents would approve of a scheme that would track children into trade and vocational programs; the white-collar model still seems to shape the parental dream, and to rule out a chance to work for a corporate bureaucracy seems foolish. Similarly most parents do not advocate a curriculum through which children sort themselves out by interest or talent, nor one that permits "electives" too far removed from the standard academic, exam-directed path. Even the mother of Toru (the pupil of *juku* teacher Sagara, described in chapter 8), who had hoped that she could raise her son free of the intense pressure of the usual curriculum, has decided to keep his chances alive within the system. In short, Japanese parents want schools to be supportive and caring, but they do not want a school to become a place where idiosyncrasy is encouraged. It falls to the media to decry conformism and "the quality-control managers called teachers who . . . treat students like cucumbers: bent cucumbers are difficult to pack with straight ones; thus idiosyncratic cucumbers are seen as abnormal."[6] This is not a live issue for most parents.

When Japanese think about educational reform, they are aware of the implicit trade-offs if they are to Westernize the school system. When Americans look at Japanese education, they would like to find a way to improve children's test scores and instill a greater sense of responsibility and discipline. When Japanese look to the West, they look for models that will provide a more expansive, liberal, individualized form of instruction and give children more room to be creative. What, then, can we learn from each other?

10

A CHOICE FOR CHILDREN

The school board chairman of one of the largest school districts in the United States once called me out of the blue. He wanted to know how many children were in an average Japanese elementary school class and what its teacher–student ratio was. I said the average class had forty-two children and one teacher. Silence on the other end of the line. The caller then composed himself and said that this wasn't the answer he wanted; he had hoped that the teacher–student ratio would be "better than that." He explained why he *needed* it to be "better." His board was campaigning to increase teacher hiring. The assumption was that the present twenty-seven students per teacher was too high and that discipline, motivation, and achievement suffered. The further assumption was that *control* was the problem—one teacher could not handle so many kids.

The chairman had heard that Japanese schoolchildren were nicely behaved, and felt sure the reason was smaller classes or more teachers in the classroom. Using what he presumed to be the Japanese model, he wanted to establish a student–teacher ratio of fifteen to one. He didn't get the news he was looking for.

Control, discipline, and ways to engage children in the classroom clearly are not always what we think they are. Americans assume that successful learning occurs in a "well-controlled" classroom, and

179

thus conclude that the Japanese classroom has to be run by a drill sergeant. The school board chairman could hardly believe that Japanese achievement has little to do with classroom orderliness and discipline, which are mostly absent, and a lot to do with high energy engagement fostered by parents, teachers, and society at large. The directed enthusiasm of a Japanese classroom is a product of the relationship between teacher and students, possible in Japan with a high student–teacher ratio, but not possible here with a much lower ratio. In short, to improve classroom performance, the Japanese and Americans may not always be able to rely on the same things.

Another recent episode also shows how we project our own assumptions about education onto the Japanese. Visiting Washington, the Japanese minister of education met with the American secretary of education, who praised Japanese schooling and exhorted Americans to borrow the key to academic achievement, "the excellent Japanese *juku* system." A shocked silence followed, after which an aide informed the secretary that it is precisely the *juku* that the ministry wants to abolish, to relieve exam pressure on Japanese children. The secretary may not have been very well briefed, but like many others, he sees in the *juku* the harnessing of effort and commitment that Americans feel our schools don't have. If we could only import the *juku,* the secretary may have felt, just as we have imported Sonys and Toyotas.

The question of what education should do affects all countries, advanced and developing. And the question of what we Americans should do usually comes down to what we should spend, with economic models holding sway: measures of input and output, of costs and benefits. The sad fact is that cultural factors are treated as exotica rather than as creative, generative influences.

And yet the environment of the school is governed by cultural values and assumptions: even the shape and visual tone of the school building speaks volumes about our attitudes toward children and learning—attitudes constrained or enhanced by holdovers from past modes. Many American children today attend school in nineteenth or early twentieth century buildings. For many contemporary observers, these symbolize obsolete, rigid, and authoritarian instruction. Japanese schools are for the most part housed in postwar buildings, not luxurious but functional. They strike Americans as drab, bare, and almost punitive, like the institutional settings of older hospitals or our own schools of the 1940s. However, as Thomas Rohlen notes: "[The Japanese] seem to want the unadorned pragmatism to be the inspiration."[1] The newer American school, of course, features color and lively design— dull linoleum floors, beige walls, and the smell of ammonia having been exiled.

The ideological context for the design of the American school is a native Calvinistic pessimism that coexists with faith in progress, a determined sort of native optimism. Our Calvinism tells us that a child's propensity for evil must be constrained; that the essence of morality is control. Meanwhile, the tradition out of Rousseau informs us that the child is innately good; that there is thus no contradiction between warm nurturance and the enhancement of a child's life chances. So what emerges from this mix? A compromise—namely, that what is innate in a child is as easily bad as good. The cheer of a newer American school may even reflect the cultural compromise. We assume that a child needs to be wooed into liking school, and color and liveliness do that.

By contrast, the postwar Japanese school is a place where no contradiction exists between a child's "nature" and a child's "training." A child can learn, wants to learn, and wants to learn in school. An upbeat, cheerful atmosphere is clearly evident without the bright and cheerful physical surroundings. Moreover, Japanese teachers don't see themselves as classroom cops. Control is, or has to be, a priority in American schools, as teachers patrol aisles and put down disruptive behavior.

American educational practice, at least in the early elementary years, seems very much taken by the idea of "whole child development"—balanced attention to affective, cognitive, and behavioral needs of the child. Classroom priorities come down hard on the side of the behavioral, though not in service to the child's development, but rather to *the teacher's need for classroom order*. Japanese priorities also regard behavioral development as important, but as Lewis and Taniuchi have shown,[2] teachers fear disruption less and worry more about a child's internalizing proper social norms.

In fact, as Taniuchi has also noted,[3] Japanese teachers are often entirely willing to treat one child's behavioral problem, even to hold up the class's activities and schedule for a considerable period of time. Thus, at the level of practice, not ideology, Americans tend to let the Calvinist side of their heritage guide events in the classroom, while the Japanese, with less ambiguity in their culture, give freer rein to the child although teacher guidance is still very much in evidence. Disparate ideologies and practices make the Japanization of any American school a tough trick.

There is a paradox and irony here. Japanese elementary school teachers usually don't find themselves laying down the law, and instead spend time trying to create ways to engage children emotionally. Their American counterparts, fully imbued with the ideals of freedom and individual expression, are preoccupied with maintaining class order and sometimes little else—as is shown in the following vignette from an American elementary school.

A few days after the *Challenger* shuttle tragedy, I was a guest at a third grade class. The teacher announced that she *had been asked* to have the children express their feelings about the disaster. She said, "Does anyone have anything to say?" Many hands were raised, and she called on students one at a time, never commenting on anything said but simply following each remark with "Next" in a flat tone. After five or six children, she looked at her watch and said, "That's all we have time for. Open your math workbooks, please."

This was a dead classroom. But a second grade teacher in another American school spent a half-hour with a group of five children in a lively and intense discussion of an exhibition they had just seen. Notable here was that the teacher did not elicit individual opinions one at a time, assuming that by doing so she had done her democratic and individualistic duty. Instead, she encouraged her students to talk *to each other,* not just to report to her. They could argue or agree as they might, and in the end they became, for a time, a group with a shared consensus instead of an aggregate of opinion holders. This was an exciting classroom moment, and, for me, evidence that teaching by our lights and traditions can work.

Fixed Potential or Unlimited Possibilities?

How do American and Japanese schools see a child's academic potential? Because the threat of bad, even violent behavior hangs over the American classroom, Americans have become increasingly pessimistic about what and how much a child can do, how much can be done to enhance development, and what standards might realistically be set for any age group. The final explanation is "innate ability,"—a notion that runs counter to deeply held American convictions about the Lockean tabula rasa, the efficacy of effort, and rising from log cabin to White House. In short, if a democratic society is open, so too are possibilities for a child's mind. Yet in pedagogical practice, there is a settled notion of fixed potential—thus the common entry on a report card reading "Works to the limit of his ability."

For the Japanese child, there are external standards to which *everyone* can in fact aspire. What counts is effort, the only constraints being physical health or the motivation provided by adults—most notably the mother. The existence of these society-wide standards, uncomplicated by great cultural diversity within the population or by great socioeconomic gaps between families, is *itself* a powerful source of motivation.

How are the Japanese standards manifested and understood by adults, and how does the child learn what is expected? There are no official guidelines for what the successful child can do at various stages, but there are curricular guidelines: what tasks ought to have been completed, what materials covered at what level. Children are measured and ranked, and there is a considerable amount of "folk" understanding of what one has to have to contend for a place at certain high schools and universities. And it is precisely that informal consensus along with specific national standards—goals, in short—that induces parents and children to work. Moreover, the countervailing emphasis on the essential *similarities* among children and a strong resistance to tracking by ability buffers competitive striving. Japanese children know what is expected of them, and they also know that to achieve it they must work hard as individuals. They know too, however, that invidious public comparisons between themselves and others who are more able will not be made in the classroom.

COOPERATION AND INDIVIDUAL IDENTITY

The Western idea of achievement is so closely tied to the ethic of individualism that it is very difficult for us to conceive of any communal definition of success as meaningful. It is "against human nature," we feel, to expect a person to work wholeheartedly for something that will not bring individual distinction or material reward. When the sixth-grader Tomoko participates in a class play, she is of course afraid that she might forget her lines and embarrass herself, but she also sincerely prays that she will do well for the sake of all the children performing in a class effort. When the high schooler

Yukio helps to organize the school's sports day, he does not expect to benefit personally, but he does expect he will contribute to the glory of the class.

What, then, is the extraordinary individual effort required to prepare for the infamous entrance examinations? How can that possibly redound to the benefit of a group? Here a subtle act of psychocultural translation is needed. Remember the attempt to define the word *sunao*. I said that the most frequent English translation, "obedient," was a serious distortion of the Japanese understanding of the term.

The fact that the word is so translated, however, gives us a way to understand how very differently the West and Japan place an individual in the social nexus. We have an individual psychology; the Japanese, the nuances and meanings of a social psychology. In other words, Western and Japanese values and goals for the individual are not the same. I said that "obedience," like "acquiescence" and "compliance," have negative or ambiguous connotations in Western child development theory. Western adults, of course, want peace and cooperation from children, and teachers especially don't want trouble with a single child's idiosyncratic "behavior problems." But the same adults, talking and thinking about children in their care, will say proudly "What a little individual he is" or "That girl is listening to a distant drummer" or "This child is a good self-starter, a leader, independent." Report cards, especially in elementary schools, are imbued with the rhetoric of individualism: "works well without direction," "initiates projects," "is an independent thinker."

Thus, to Western ears, obedience is a necessary evil and implies a trade-off: the adult has *forced* the child to submit, to sacrifice some of his precious autonomy for the needs of the social group—needs that are not in themselves especially valued. Necessary submission provides the minimal conditions under which "society" can operate—just enough law, order, and structure. Meantime, there is no invasion of anyone's territory, no preemption of individual rights, no destruction of autonomy or wounding of ego. Obedience is seen as the offspring of authoritarianism, and Western social and political ideas and ideals abhor the hierarchies and absolutism implied by authority. The notions of Rousseau and Dewey fully reflect modern Western conceptions of childhood and society—remove chains that bind and abolish hierarchy. As for Japanese educators, they took to the idea of both men that the child is innately good.

The conceptual paradox in Western child development theory is that even while giving the child (at least on paper) unrestrained freedom, educators were not entirely sure that they weren't thereby opening Pandora's box. And out of that box would come the child's primitive and essential badness. In fact, the tension between the happy pastoral and the primal passions of the juvenile id has never for us been resolved.

Thus, when we translate *sunao* as "obedient," we project our notions of authority and our idea of an innate capacity for evil onto the Japanese child. A more accurate translation of the term is "cooperative as an act of confirmation of the self." Hence, a *sunao* child is a good participant in group activities, a good listener to adults, a good replicator of society's norms and standards. Being all these things makes him feel accomplished and enhances his identity—his most profoundly personal "self."

We must understand this human reality if we are to see how even the entrance exams, study for which ultimately isolates an individual Japanese child, represent not only a personal triumph or disappointment but also the deeply embedded human relationships of families, peer groups, and school classes. So it is no wonder that the Japanese feel that "examination hell" comes not only from the pressure to study but also from the effects of social isolation, individualism, and other excesses of competition. Under less extreme conditions, the pressure to study is fully supported and cushioned by the network of human relationships that form all of the groups to which the Japanese child belongs.

Japanese children are always assured of support, exhortation, and devotion from their parents, school, and the society at large, but especially from their mothers. Remember Keiko, the mother of the nursery schooler Kenichi. In no way begrudging the emotional commitment required, she expects to shape her days around him for many years, and in the expectation, she is herself part of a consensus that mothering so understood is an appropriate and essential focus for a woman's life. For without such mothering, it is understood within the Japanese cultural unconscious that both the future of children and the survival of the nation are imperiled.

So the time she spends with her child she regards as time indistinguishable from time for herself. For most Japanese women, problems arise only when they do anything—work or a hobby—that might conflict with mothering. This incurs social opprobrium. Western mothers often say that getting away from their children (whether by working or just having "time for themselves") is a good thing: first, because they believe that children thereby become more independent; and second, because they believe that a woman who has an identity independent of the home is a happier person and therefore a less frustrated and better mother.

Studies purporting to measure satisfaction find Japanese women "more satisfied" than Western women with their lives. But attitude studies like this can scarcely be taken at face value, and in no way should be read to mean that Western women would be happier if they became more like Japanese women. As Thomas Jefferson may have understood, the pursuit of happiness varies from man to man, woman to woman, and culture to culture.

THE CHOICE FOR CHILDREN

While cries and alarms have been sounded in the United States, summoning experts and policymakers to the pedagogical war-rooms, Western interest in education may finally not be about children, but about a kind of face-saving nationalism to compensate for loss of economic competitiveness. Hence we see a level of anxiety about schooling reminiscent of the years after the Sputnik launchings.

The language used by the West toward Japan is not just protectionist, but recently positively belligerent. In 1985, for example, Theodore White wrote an almost hysterical piece in the *New York Times* about Japan's coming economic hegemony. He warned the Japanese that "we have not forgotten Pearl Harbor."[4]

Educators are milder people. Some have tied Japanese economic success to exertions made in behalf of education, but few claim that a Japanese child's test scores portend evidence of new Japanese imperial aggression. Or perhaps something other than reasonableness keeps Western observers of Japanese schools from calling out the curricular marines. It may be that, after all, our sense of life does not in any fundamental way link the formal education system to social and economic welfare; maybe we really do not believe that what a child learns in school affects what he becomes later or our society's strength and stature generally.

This cannot be the case in Japan, for it must depend on its schools to develop its most important resource—children. Their education, therefore, is a top national priority, expressed and acted upon from the highest levels down. This reinforces the already existing commitment felt by individual parents; so by personal and social attitudes and by institutional emphasis Japanese education gets a high public profile. Elsewhere regarded as a "soft" issue, education in Japan is a concern which even the most macho political leader sees as critical. Having status and clout, the needs of children and schools have complete access to those in the halls of power. As Thomas Rohlen says, the Japanese see education as "shaping a national citizenry,"[5] and it is therefore a national concern. I see Japanese educational mobilization as coming from a confluence of the traditional, deep-seated national preoccupation with resource scarcity, on the one hand, and equally deep personal, parental interest in children, on the other. Mobilization is both top-down and bottom-up, highly conscious of itself and powerful.

Western parents also, of course, feel that their children's education is very important—even in the United States, where academic achievement is not seen to determine a person's life chances. In any case, we like to think of ourselves as good parents; and we are, by our own lights and on our own terms, though we vary by culture, class, and region. We care for our children physically; buy them the best we can afford in food, clothing, and toys; send them to camp and music lessons; help them to manage their lives in ways we consider healthy, satisfying, and constructive. Occasionally we mobilize collectively to protect our children from traffic, molestation, television, drugs, pollution, or junk food. We rarely, however, bestir ourselves beyond the local community to reach national institutions for the benefit of children. We may in fact find it easier to work for children in drought-stricken Africa than to commit ourselves to the long-term and less dramatic needs of children in our society.

The conclusion is that we need to be more than good parents to our own children. We have to resist the fashionable privatism and decentralization that erode the consensus for change which now exists. We have to link our private interest in our own offspring to a national program of commitment to enhance the lives of all American children.

We have done and will do things differently from the Japanese. We will most probably not institute an intensive examination system, for we will persist, correctly I think, in the notion that nobody's chances in life should be determined by a few hours sitting in an examination room. Our society must remain at least as open as it is today, for that is one of our great strengths. In addition, we can never expect Western mothers to dedicate their lives to helping their children stay afloat in an educational system such as the Japanese have.

We have much to learn from the Japanese, however, about commitment and effort. Some of our athletes and musicians already exhibit a Japanese level of intensity. So we can do it, even though our society does not value endurance for its own sake. Knowing what the Japanese do, we might also begin to ask more from children, parents, teachers, and schools. Expectations matter. We should give academic subjects priority, and rid schools of silly electives that may make being there superficially palatable but waste children's time. The same energy sometimes given to frills might be devoted to engaging children in basic subjects.

Knowing what the Japanese do, we should work to make school a more legitimate place for teachers to work. To do that we must first enhance their lives, roles, and capacities. Japanese and European teachers have more confidence in their specialities than do American teachers, who have spent too much time in courses on pedagogy and curriculum. European and Japanese teachers also receive more respect in the community than do American teachers. Ours nearly always enter the profession hoping to go on to something better, and they often do.

Respect is reflected in salary. Japanese teachers earn more on entry than other civil servants in Japan, and their starting salaries equal or better those in large companies. Teaching is a sought-after and rewarding career for college graduates; American teachers earn the least of all college graduates.

In short, we must make schools places where both students and teachers can find what our society genuinely regards as important, constructive, and motivating. Everybody then benefits. There are no magic-wand solutions, but we may perhaps formulate some thoughtful compromises which will soften the harshness and dissonance of our educational paradoxes. We need explicit standards for children's academic performance—but we need also to serve the diversity of potential among them; we need to maintain tougher academic standards—but we need also to eschew alienating and invidious distinctions between advantage and disadvantage; we need to do much more for our teachers—but we of course can't keep them from moving on to better things; we need to engage parents more fully in the schooling of their children—but we need also to protect the educational system from the political and debilitating effects of serving multiple constituencies. This last is a hard one in our pluralistic society, which both values and contends with diversity.

Finally, we need to try to motivate children through care and support, and not try to control them through fear. The American school board chairperson learned that Japanese teachers, with large classes, don't spend much time *controlling* students' behavior. So the purely quantitative often misleads: our 28:1 student–teacher ratio versus their 42:1 ratio, or our 180 school days versus their 240 days. The cultural environment is the significant factor in Japanese educational success, and of course it cannot be duplicated elsewhere in wholesale fashion. But I am convinced that Dallas and Boston, London and Manchester, Paris and Lyon, given sufficient commitment, can develop productive indigenous cultural frameworks that will help children learn—so long as none use the school to serve agendas that don't serve children. The issue in fact is what we really want for our children and how hard we are willing to work for it.

We are, I will say confidently, better off without Japan's examination system, which can easily distort what children should learn in secondary education, and which for some leads to personal disaster. But we still need the national standards the exams represent, the impetus they give to parents to work with their children, the academic focus they provide. The problem for all of us is how we can get clear focus and intense motivation without having to face an eventual do-or-die moment of testing.

We are also better off without the single-track mode of Japanese education. Young people like Yukio, good at math but not interested in much else, would do better in our system, which would let him excel where he wanted to. In any case, Japanese cultural homogeneity is not a possibility for us, nor do we want the way we live monitored by community vigilance—the *seken*. For better or for worse, we are a motley nation and need a greater, wider range of permitted norms.

There is an aspect of Japanese education that may suit us, work for us, even as we find it appealing. This is Japanese elementary school education. The system has produced some very notable achievements—chief among them, thoroughly motivated children fully engaged in learning. Here cramming for exams has not yet created the kind of anxiety that we would find unacceptable in our schools. The elementary school successfully engenders good habits and a positive outlook, helping to create a noncompetitive personal drive in older children, and the confidence among all the children that they *can* learn hard things. All this produces children who are able not only to survive later educational trials, but to triumph over them. There is no question that Japanese psychocultural means are used to develop these desirable ends of Japanese elementary school education. But I strongly feel that if desired ends are shared, Westerners can find the appropriate means within their own traditions to reach them. However, we can get there only if we can tap indigenous roots. Understood this way, Japanese education has no secrets that can be whispered to us.

Accordingly, we want for our children some of the things Japanese children get, but not all of what they get. I think we approve of the human warmth found in the toddler Kenichi's environment. We also like the uncomplicated joy evident in Jiro's and Tomoko's elementary schools. The lives of Yukio and Nobuya represent problematic cases. And we would put our high school children at risk if only a *juku* teacher like Sagara could "rescue" a youth like Toru from potential failure.

The Japanese, too, are not sure they want to move in our direction, however attractive the abstract notions of freedom and creative exploration may sound. But should they decide to move our way, I would guess they have a better chance of taking a centralized, focused system and developing areas of freedom than we have of creating a sense of direction from anarchy. The Japanese have another advantage, which they have used well in past borrowings from the West. They are alert to the need to maintain their own cultural values and practices at the core of any new system adopted. They regard culture as an integral, dynamic part of their society and economy. For Americans bred on Adam Smith and Thomas Jefferson, culture is what's left only after the market economy and attendant social mobility have worked their will.

And we shouldn't complacently assert that they can't do what *we* can do; namely, win Nobel prizes and innovate in basic research. They *can* do it, and have recently established a society-wide consensus to push the need for creativity. So even on the frontiers of science, we face a mobilized Japan. Everybody knows that the United States and Japan compete on any number of industrial fronts and everybody should be more straightforward about it: there is a lot of money—or put euphemistically, market share—on the table, and one competitor could easily walk away with what the other would regard as the fruits of cheating. We can only hope to do what we do well, and do it better. The same goes for the Japanese, though both sides will still feel that what the other side does better is unfair and duplicitous.

Meanwhile, the challenge inherent in the Japanese school is a clear demonstration of the power of cultural consensus and of being true to one's roots. If we want to borrow anything from the Japanese, it is, paradoxically, the attention they devote to their *own* paramount cultural priority: the improvement of children's lives. If we don't have such a priority, we must make it our cultural and parental responsibility to develop one.

Notes

Introduction (pp. 1–8)

1. In this book, the pronouns *he/him/his* are used generically to refer to both males and females.

Chapter 1. Resources and Mobilization (pp. 11–19)

1. Sumiko Iwao, "Skills and Life Strategies of Japanese Businesswomen," in *The Cultural Transition: Human Experience and Social Transformation in the Third World and Japan,* ed. Merry White and Susan Pollak (London: Routledge & Kegan Paul, 1986).
2. Ibid., 242.
3. Hidetoshi Kato, "The Japanese in the World Today," Tokyo Kaigi, conference sponsored by the *Yomiuri Shimbun,* Oct. 1985, page 2.
4. *Course of Study in Elementary Schools in Japan* (Tokyo: Ministry of Education, 1983), 111.
5. Ibid., 116.

Chapter 2. Motivation and Mores (pp. 20–49)

1. Takeo Doi, *The Anatomy of Dependence* (Tokyo: Kodansha, 1973), 7.
2. William Caudill and Helen Weinstein, "Maternal Care and Infant Behavior in Japan and America," *Psychiatry* 32, no. 1 (1969): 12–43.

3. Irene Shigaki, "Child Care Practices in Japan and the U.S.," *Young Children* 38, no. 4 (May 1983).

4. Thomas Rohlen, *Japan's High Schools* (Berkeley: University of California Press, 1983), 314.

5. Howard Gardner, *Frames of Mind* (New York: Basic Books, 1983), 237 ff.

6. Hisa Kumagai, "A Dissection of Intimacy: A Study of 'Bipolar Posturing' in Japanese Social Interaction—*Amaeru* and *Amayakasu*, Indulgence and Deference," *Culture, Medicine and Psychiatry* 5 (1981): 249–272.

7. Ibid., 261.

8. Lois Taniuchi Peak, "The Psychological Transition from Home to School and the Development of Japanese Children's Attitudes Towards Learning," unpublished qualifying paper, Harvard Graduate School of Education, Aug. 1982.

9. Mary Conroy, Robert Hess, Hiroshi Azuma, and Keiko Kashiwagi, "Maternal Strategies for Regulating Children's Behavior," *Journal of Cross-Cultural Psychology* 11, no. 2 (June 1980): 153–172.

10. M. Yamazuni and K. Nakae, *Kosodate no sho*, vol. 1 (Tokyo: Heibonsha, 1976).

11. John Singleton, "*Gambaru:* A Japanese Cultural Theory of Learning," in *Society, Equality and Politics in Japanese Schooling*, ed. James Shields (Pittsburgh: University of Pittsburgh Press, forthcoming).

12. Ruth Benedict, *The Chrysanthemum and the Sword* (Boston: Houghton Mifflin Co., 1946).

13. Helmut Morsbach, "Sociopsychological Aspects of Persistence in Japan," in *Essays on Japanology, 1978–1982* (Kyoto: Bunrikaku, 1983), 12.

14. Ibid., 12.

15. TDK Corporation, *Our School*, Teachers' Guide (New York: The Asia Society, 1985), 17.

16. Morsbach, 20.

17. Singleton.

18. Perry Garfinkel, "The Best Jewish Mother in the World," *Psychology Today* 17 (September 1983): 56–60.

19. Shigefumi Nagano, cited in discussion held at Project on Human Potential, Harvard Graduate School of Education, May 1982.

20. *Asahi Shimbun*, May 10, 1985, p. 21; May 29, 1985, p. 12.

Chapter 3. Japanese Schools: Perspectives from History
(*pp. 50–65*)

1. George deVos, cited in Richard K. Beardsley, John W. Hall, and Robert E. Ward, *Village Japan* (Chicago: University of Chicago Press, 1959), 68.

2. Herbert Passin, cited in Marius Jansen and Lawrence Stone, "Education and Modernization in Japan and England," *Comparative Studies in Society and History* 9, no. 2 (Jan. 1967).

3. Cited in Herbert Passin, *Society and Education in Japan* (New York: Teachers College Press, 1967), 22.

4. Yukichi Fukuzawa, *The Autobiography of Yukichi Fukuzawa* (New York: Schocken Books, 1972), 22.

5. Ibid., 13.

6. Mikiso Hane, *Peasants, Rebels and Outcasts: The Underside of Modern Japan* (New York: Pantheon Press, 1982) and Thomas Havens, *The Valley of Darkness* (New York: Norton, 1978).

7. Gunzo Kojima, *Philosophical Foundations for Democratic Education in Japan* (Tokyo: International Christian University, 1959), 96–97.

Chapter 4. Japanese Schools Today (pp. 66–81)

1. Joseph Jay Tobin, Dana H. Davidson, and David Y. H. Wu, "Ratios and Class Size in the Japanese Preschool," unpublished manuscript, 1985.

2. Sheppard Ranbom, "Schooling in Japan," *Education Week* (three-part article: Feb. 20, Feb. 27, March 6, 1985).

3. Merry White and Lois Taniuchi, "Teaching and Learning in Japan," unpublished paper prepared for Project on Human Potential, Harvard Graduate School of Education, 1982.

4. Harold Stevenson, "Classroom Behavior and Achievement of Japanese, Chinese and American Children," in *Child Development and Education in Japan*, ed. Hiroshi Azuma, Harold Stevenson, and Kenji Hakuta (New York: Freeman Press, 1986).

5. L. C. Comber and John P. Keeves, *Science Achievement in Nineteen Countries* (New York: John Wiley & Sons, 1973); Torsten Husen, *International Study of Achievement in Math: A Comparison of Twelve Countries*, vol. 2 (New York: John Wiley & Sons, 1967).

6. Rohlen, 296.

7. White and Taniuchi.

8. The following section is drawn from White and Taniuchi.

9. Diane Ravitch, "Japan's Smart Schools," *New Republic*, Jan. 13, 1986, pp. 13–15.

Chapter 5. A Paradise for Teachers? (pp. 82–91)

1. William Cummings, *Education and Equality in Japan* (Princeton, N.J.: Princeton University Press, 1980).

2. Rohlen, 177.

3. John Singleton, *Nichuu* (New York: Holt, Rinehart & Winston, 1966).

4. Cummings.

Chapter 6. *Learning at Mother's Knee* (pp. 95–109)

1. Merry White and Lois Taniuchi, "The Anatomy of the *Hara*," unpublished paper written for the Project on Human Potential, Harvard Graduate School of Education, 1980.

2. Betty Lanham, "Aspects of Child Care in Japan: Preliminary Report," in *Personal Character and Cultural Milieu,* ed. D. G. Haring (Syracuse N.Y.: Syracuse University Press, 1956), 581.

3. Eugen Herrigel, *Zen and the Art of Archery* (New York: Vintage Press, 1953).

4. Michael Kirst, "Japanese Education: Its Implications for Economic Cooperation in the 1980s," *Phi Delta Kappan* (June 1981): 708.

5. Nishinomiya Pre-School Education Study Group, "Report on Pre-school Education" (Nishinomiya: March 1983).

6. Japan. Ministry of Education, *Statistical Abstract of Education, Science and Culture.* Tokyo, 1983, p. 36 ff.

7. Catherine C. Lewis, "Cooperation and Control in Japanese Nursery Schools," *Comparative Education Review* 28, no. 1 (Feb. 1984).

8. Lois Taniuchi Peak, "The Psychological Transition from Home to School and the Development of Japanese Children's Attitudes Towards Learning," unpublished paper, Harvard Graduate School of Education, 1982.

9. Thomas Rohlen, *For Harmony and Strength* (Berkeley: University of California Press, 1974).

10. Lewis (op. cit.) and Peak (op. cit.).

11. Lois Taniuchi, "Cultural Continuity in an Educational Institution: A Case Study of the Suzuki Method of Music Instruction," in *The Cultural Transition: Human Experience and Social Transformation in the Third World,* ed. Merry White and Susan Pollak (London: Routledge & Kegan Paul, 1986).

Chapter 7. *Elementary Schools* (pp. 110–133)

1. Lois Taniuchi Peak, "The Psychological Transition from Home to School," 1982.

2. The similarity between this kind of classroom and a typical office is striking. Such an office is a large open room with many desks facing one another in rows, allowing everyone to be part of an active, usually fairly noisy environment. As in the classroom, productivity and "health" are measured by the visible and audible evidence of engagement.

3. Another example illustrates school, rather than class, uniformity. On the day when national achievement tests were given, a school requested that those children who were near failure stay home and not take the test, so that the school's record would not be blemished.

4. Cummings, 127.

5. Esther Kohn, "Beyond the Self: Group Learning in Japan," unpublished manuscript, Harvard Graduate School of Education, spring 1985.

6. Letter from John Dewey, cited in Victor N. Kobayashi, *John Dewey in Japanese Educational Thought* (Ann Arbor: University of Michigan Press, 1964), 28.

7. Gary Swartz, "Wilf's School," *PHP* (Aug. 1984): 30–38.

8. It is interesting to consider the differences in audiences for these goods in Japan and the United States. Originating in Japan, under such labels as Hello Kitty, and Patty and Jimmy, these items were seen as excellent exports to the American market. In Japan they sell to girls from ten to twenty years of age, and in fact, to girls of almost any age before marriage. When performing a market analysis of the appropriate American audience for these "cute" things, the American researchers advised companies that the appropriate age group in America was girls aged four to seven. I am grateful to Liza Crihfield Dalby for this comment.

9. Rohlen, *Japan's High Schools,* 196.

Chapter 8. Secondary Schools (*pp. 134–162*)

1. Boston *Globe,* June 28, 1985, p. 67. Reprinted courtesy of The Boston Globe.

2. Margaret Lock, "Plea for Acceptance: School Refusal Syndrome in Japan," unpublished paper presented at Association for Asian Studies Annual Meeting, Philadelphia, March 1985.

3. Donald Roden, *Schooldays in Imperial Japan* (Berkeley: University of California Press, 1980).

4. *Wall Street Journal,* Nov. 12, 1985.

5. *Far Eastern Economic Review,* May 23, 1985, p. 66.

6. Miyazaki Ichisaka, *China's Examination Hell,* trans. Conrad Shirokauer (New Haven: Yale University Press, 1981).

7. Ronald Dore, *The Diploma Disease* (Berkeley: University of California Press, 1976).

8. Thomas Rohlen, "Is Japanese Education Becoming Less Egalitarian? Notes on Stratification and Reform," *Journal of Japanese Studies* (winter 1976–77).

9. Dore, *The Diploma Disease,* 49.

10. Ibid., 50.

11. Rohlen, *Japan's High Schools,* 195–196.

12. *Nichibei Seinen Hikaku Chosa Hokokusho* (Report on Comparative Study of Youth in the U.S.A. and Japan) (Tokyo: Nihon Seinen Kenkyusho, 1979).

13. Harold Stevenson, James W. Stigler, and Shin-ying Lee, "Achievement in Mathematics" in *Child's development and education in Japan,* ed. Hiroshi Azuma, Kenji Hakuta, and Harold Stevenson (New York: Freeman, 1986), 203–204.

Chapter 9. Japan in Transition (*pp. 165–178*)

1. Stevenson.

2. Rohlen, *Japan's High Schools,* 108–109.

3. Tetsuko Kuroyanagi, *Totto-chan: The Little Girl at the Window,* trans. Dorothy Britton (Tokyo: Kodansha, 1982).

4. Hiroshi Kida, discussion at National Institute for Educational Research, Tokyo, May 17, 1982.

5. Ikuo Amano, ''The Socio-political Background of the Educational Crisis in Japan,'' unpublished paper presented at ''Learning from Each Other: A Comparison of U.S. and Japanese Education'' (Honolulu, Aug. 24–27, 1984), 32.

6. *Asahi Shimbun* article quoted in ''The unfortunate victims of Japan's classroom bullies,'' *Far Eastern Economic Review,* May 23, 1985, pp. 65–66.

Chapter 10. A Choice for Children (pp. 179–191)

1. Rohlen, *Japan's High Schools,* 146.

2. Lewis (1984) and Taniuchi, 1982.

3. Ibid.

4. Theodore White, ''The Danger from Japan,'' *New York Times,* July 28, 1985.

5. Rohlen, *Japan's High Schools,* 2.

Bibliography

Amano, Ikuo. "The Socio-political Background of the Educational Crisis in Japan." Unpublished paper presented at "Learning from Each Other: A Comparison of U.S. and Japanese Education," Honolulu, Aug. 24–27. 1984.

Anderson, Ronald. *Education in Japan.* Washington, D.C.: U.S. Government Printing Office, 1974.

Azuma, Hiroshi, Kenji Hakuta, and Harold Stevenson. *Child Development and Education in Japan.* New York: Freeman, 1986.

Beardsley, Richard K., John W. Hall, and Robert E. Ward. *Village Japan.* Chicago: University of Chicago Press, 1959.

Benedict, Ruth. *The Chrysanthemum and the Sword.* Boston: Houghton Mifflin Co., 1946.

Caudill, William. "Tiny Dramas: Verbal Communication Between Mother and Infant in Japanese and American families." In *Transcultural Research in Mental Health,* edited by William Lebra. Honolulu: University of Hawaii Press, 1972.

———, and Helen Weinstein. "Maternal Care and Infant Behavior in Japan and America." *Psychiatry* 32, no. 1 (1969): 12–43.

Comber, L. C., and John P. Keeves. *Science Achievement in Nineteen Countries,* New York: John Wiley & Sons, 1973.

Conroy, Mary, Robert Hess, Hiroshi Azuma, and Keiko Kashiwagi. "Maternal Strategies for Regulating Children's Behavior." *Journal of Cross-cultural Psychology,* 11, no. 2 (June 1980): 153–172.

Cummings, William. *Education and Equality in Japan.* Princeton, N.J.: Princeton University Press, 1980.

Dahrendorf, Ralf. *Life Chances,* Chicago: University of Chicago Press, 1978.

Doi, Takeo. *The Anatomy of Dependence.* Tokyo: Kodansha, 1973.

Dore, Ronald. *The Diploma Disease.* Berkeley: University of California Press, 1976.

———. *Education in Tokugawa Japan.* Berkeley: University of California Press, 1965.

———. *City Life in Japan.* Berkeley: University of California Press, 1958.

Far Eastern Economic Review. "The Unfortunate Victims of Japan's Classroom Bullies," May 23, 1985, pp. 65–66.

Fukuzawa, Yukichi. *The Autobiography of Yukichi Fukuzawa.* New York: Schocken Books, 1972.

Gardner, Howard. *Frames of Mind.* New York: Basic Books, 1983.

Garfinkel, Perry. "The Best Jewish Mother in the World." *Psychology Today* 17 (Sept. 1983): 56–60.

Hane, Mikiso. *Peasants, Rebels and Outcastes: The Underside of Modern Japan.* New York: Pantheon Press, 1982.

Havens, Thomas. *The Valley of Darkness: The Japanese People and World War II.* New York: Norton, 1978.

Herrigel, Eugen. *Zen and the Art of Archery.* New York: Vintage Press, 1953.

Hess, Robert, Keiko Kashiwagi, and Hiroshi Azuma. "Maternal Expectations for Mastery of Developmental Tasks in Japan and the U.S." *International Journal of Psychology* 15 (1980): 259–271.

Husen, Torsten. *International Study of Achievement in Math: A Comparison of Twelve Countries.* Vol. 2. New York: John Wiley & Sons, 1967.

Inagaki, Tadahiko. "Education in Japan from a Comparative Point of View." Unpublished paper prepared for "Learning from Each Other: A Comparison of U.S. and Japanese Education," Honolulu, Aug. 24–27, 1984.

Iwao, Sumiko. "Skills and Strategies of Japanese Businesswomen." In *The Cultural Transition: Human Experience and Social Transformation in the Third World and Japan,* edited by Merry White and Susan Pollak. London: Routledge & Kegan Paul, 1986.

Jansen, Marius, and Lawrence Stone "Education and Modernization in Japan and England." *Comparative Studies in Society and History,* 9, no. 2 (Jan. 1967).

Japan. Ministry of Education. *Course of Study for Elementary Schools.* Tokyo, 1985.

———. *Statistical Abstract of Education, Science and Culture.* Tokyo, 1983.

———. *Survey on Schools.* Tokyo, Aug. 1984.

———. National Institute for Educational Research, Tokyo. *Basic Facts and Figures About the Educational System in Japan.* Tokyo, 1982.

Kato, Hidetoshi. "The Japanese in the World Today." Tokyo Kaigi, conference sponsored by the *Yomiuri Shimbun,* Oct. 1985.

Kirst, Michael. "Japanese Education: Its Implications for Economic Cooperation in the 1980s." *Phi Delta Kappan* (June 1981): 708.

Kobayashi, Victor N. *John Dewey in Japanese Educational Thought.* Ann Arbor: University of Michigan Press, 1964.

Kohn, Esther. "Beyond the Self: Group Learning in Japan." Unpublished paper, Harvard Graduate School of Education, spring 1985.

Kojima, Gunzo. *Philosophical Foundations for Democratic Education in Japan.* Tokyo: International Christian University, 1959.

Kumagai, Hisa. "A Dissection of Intimacy: A Study of Bipolar Posturing in Japanese Social Interaction—*Amaeru* and *Amayakasu,* Indulgence and Deference." *Culture, Medicine and Psychiatry* 5 (1981): 249–272.

Kuroyanagi, Tetsuko. *Totto-chan: The Little Girl at the Window.* Translated by Dorothy Britton. Tokyo: Kodansha, 1982.

Lanham, Betty. "Aspects of Child Care in Japan: Preliminary Report." In *Personal Character and Cultural Milieu,* edited by D. G. Haring. Syracuse, N.Y.: Syracuse University Press, 1956.

———. "Early Socialization: Stability and Change." In *The Study of Japan in the Behavioral Sciences,* edited by E. Norbeck and D. Parman. Rice University Studies 56, no. 4 (fall 1970).

Lewis, Catherine. "Cooperation and Control in Japanese Nursery Schools." *Comparative Education Review* 28, no. 1 (Feb. 1984).

Lock, Margaret. "Plea for Acceptance: School Refusal Syndrome in Japan." Unpublished paper presented at Association for Asian Studies Annual Meeting, Philadelphia, March 1985.

Miyazaki, Ichisaka. *China's Examination Hell.* Translated by Conrad Shirokauer. New Haven: Yale University Press, 1981.

Morsbach, Helmut. "Sociopsychological Aspects of Persistence in Japan." In *Essays on Japanology, 1978–1982.* Kyoto: Bunrikaku, 1983.

Murthy, P. A. N. *The Rise of Modern Nationalism in Japan.* New Delhi: Ashajanak, 1973.

Nichibei Seinen Hikaku Chosa Hokokusho (Report on Comparative Study of Youth in the U.S.A. and Japan) (Tokyo: Nihon Seinen Kenkyusho, 1979).

Passin, Herbert. *Society and Education in Japan.* New York: Teachers College Press, 1965.

Peak, Lois (*see also* Taniuchi, Lois).

Peak, Lois Taniuchi. "The Psychological Transition from Home to School and the Development of Children's Attitudes Towards Learning." Unpublished qualifying paper, Harvard Graduate School of Education, Aug. 1982.

Ranbom, Sheppard. "Schooling in Japan." *Education Week* (three-part article: Feb. 20, Feb. 27, March 6, 1985).

Ravitch, Diane. "Japan's Smart Schools." *New Republic,* Jan. 13, 1986.

Roden, Donald. *Schooldays in Imperial Japan.* Berkeley: University of California Press, 1980.

Rohlen, Thomas. *Japan's High Schools.* Berkeley: University of California Press, 1983.

———. "Is Japanese Education Becoming Less Egalitarian? Notes on Stratification and Reform." *Journal of Japanese Studies* (winter 1976–77).

————. *For Harmony and Strength*. Berkeley: University of California Press, 1974.

Shigaki, Irene. "Child Care Practices in Japan and the U.S.: How Do They Reflect Cultural Values in Young Children?" 38, no. 4 (May 1983).

Sikkema, Mildred. "Observations of Japanese Early Childhood Training." In *Personal Character and Cultural Milieu,* edited by D. G. Haring. Syracuse, N.Y.: Syracuse University Press, 1948.

Singleton, John. *Nichuu.* New York: Holt, Rinehart & Winston, 1966.

————. "*Gambaru:* A Japanese Cultural Theory of Learning." In *Society, Equality and Politics in Japanese Schooling,* edited by James Shields. Pittsburgh: University of Pittsburgh Press, forthcoming.

Stevenson, Harold. "Classroom Behavior and Achievement of Japanese, Chinese and American Children." In *Child Development and Education in Japan,* edited by Hiroshi Azuma, Harold Stevenson, and Kenji Hakuta. New York: Freeman, 1986.

Swartz, Gary. "Wilf's School." *PHP* (Aug. 1984).

Taniuchi, Lois. "Cultural Continuity in an Educational Institution: A Case Study of the Suzuki Method of Music Instruction." In *The Cultural Transition: Human Experience and Social Transformation in the Third World and Japan,* edited by Merry White and Susan Pollak. London: Routledge & Kegan Paul, 1986.

TDK Corporation. *Our School.* Video Letter and Teachers' Guide. New York: The Asia Society, 1985.

White, Merry, and Lois Taniuchi. "The Anatomy of the *Hara.*" Unpublished manuscript prepared for Project on Human Potential, Harvard Graduate School of Education, 1980.

————. "Teaching and Learning in Japan." Unpublished manuscript prepared for Project on Human Potential, Harvard Graduate School of Education, 1982.

White, Theodore. "The Danger from Japan." *New York Times,* July 28, 1985.

INDEX

DATE DUE